The Purposes of God and the True Basis of Redemption

The Purposes of God and the True Basis of Redemption

Arthur P. Adams (1845-1925)

BIBLE STUDENT'S PRESS™

Windber, Pennsylvania

The Purposes of God and the True Basis of Redemption
by Arthur P. Adams (1845-1925)

Original Printing: 1885

(Edited and abridged with changes to punctuation and grammar for better reading.)

Executive Editor: André Sneidar
Layout and Design: Great Adventure in Faith

Cover design by Clyde L. Pilkington, III

ASIN: B00430BI7C

Published by:
Bible Student's Press™
An imprint of *Pilkington & Sons*
  P.O. Box 265
  Windber, PA 15963
  1-800-784-6010

For information on *Bible Student's Press*™ releases, visit
  www.BibleStudentsPress.com

For information on other Bible study resources, visit
  www.StudyShelf.com

Printed in the United States of America.

CONTENTS

Chapter 1

The Purpose in Creation

The heavens declare the glory of God; and the firmament shows His handiwork.

~ Psalms 19:1

*I*n creation God gives outwardness, existence, to the highest thoughts of His mind. Everything in creation expresses a divine thought: the divine thought is its spirit, that is, its real, true meaning in the economy of God, and to apprehend that spirit is to recognize God in His works, and to recognize or know God is life. Thus creation is always consummated in *life*. That is its end.

The purpose of such creation ever and always, in the last analysis, is life; and since the highest life, or perhaps we can better understand it if we say the highest *living*, is that of the Creator Himself, hence all creation tends to bring us to the life of the Creator. Thus in an endless but ever-widening circle does God express Himself in creation that man may at the last receive His exact impress. It was only by going out of Himself, so to speak, that God could ever bring man *into* Himself.

DIVINE THOUGHT AND REVELATION

Everything in creation expresses a divine thought, and this divine thought is its spirit or true meaning in God's universe. In other words everything is a revelation of God, which proposition necessarily follows from the great truth we have already learned that God is in everything, or *"all things are of God"* (II Corinthians 5:18).

Everything in nature reveals God: every rock, every blade of grass, every plant, the very weeds that grow in our gardens as well as the grander and mightier works of nature. I cannot think that anything is so small or so insignificant that its existence is purposeless. Whatever *is, is* for a purpose, and that purpose is God's thought in its creation. There is something of God in all things, and that is its spirit.

So, too, all truth and knowledge is of God whether it be the truths of mathematics or of revelation, or whether it be the knowledge of how to tell the age of a horse by looking into his mouth, or the knowledge that fits the saint to *"judge angels"* as in I Corinthians 6:3.

Thus all truth is sacred. He who plies a mechanical trade, or fills a school-teacher's place, or honestly endeavors to alleviate the physical sufferings of his fellows, is engaged in a work as holy as he who preaches the gospel. All of truth in every department should be pursued with the object to *"find out God"* (Job 11:7). When it is thus sought the secular and the sacred will be blended into one, and head and heart shall be united.

WHAT IS TRUTH?

Pilate asked the question of Him Who *is* the Truth, *"What is truth?"* – but he did not wait for an answer, because he was not *"of the truth."* An exhaustive answer to Pilate's question would be *knowledge of God*. All truth, abstract or concrete, is *knowledge of God* in nature, or in providence, or in grace – the lowest and simplest truth as well as the highest and most profound. To the one who realizes this, everything that comes to him and all things around him are a continual surprise and delight, a perfect transcript (so far as he can understand it) of the divine mind. He walks through the world with sandals removed, as treading on holy ground, everywhere stamped with the footprints of the Creator and with head uncovered as one who at any turn may meet God.

With many Christians their religion is something entirely external; it is not a life, but is simply a dress or a cloak. To such ones God is far off. He is not available for help and counsel and guidance in ordinary matters. He is a Being Whom they must approach only at stated intervals, and with a solemn face and a particular attitude.

The religious life of such a one is exceedingly strained and artificial. There is altogether too much self-consciousness and too much regard for the *proprieties* of the occasion. We have read perhaps how children of some earthly monarch visit their parents at stated times. A certain hour of the day or week is set apart for the ceremony. The royal parents are seated in state. The children, accompanied by their nurses and attendants and dressed with great precision, appear and, advancing to the king and queen, kneel and kiss their hands, and after a few formal words they retire, all the time preserving an air of great gravity and decorum. In about the same way do very many Christians hold themselves toward their heavenly Father. If their religion does not creep, it struts, and that is worse. Approach to God becomes an unusual and a state occasion. Certain ceremonies and solemnities must always be resorted to, and the whole affair is made a matter of form and conventionality.

Now, all of this simply shows how artificial and unreal their religious life is; or rather it shows that their religion is not life at all, but merely an outside garment to be put on for particular occasions, and, when the occasion is past, to be laid aside entirely until another such occasion.

What then is the real life of such ones? You will not find out by calling on them or by meeting them occasionally in a prayer meeting or a social gathering. On such occasions also they have a garment which completely disguises the real life. Yet go and live with them every day in the week for a year: in the kitchen, in the nursery, and in all of the household cares and duties, or on the street, in the work shop, in the counting room, and amid all of the intricacies and perplexities of business life. What for? To discover their faults and failings? Bless you, no. You had better not look for *them,* lest you be put to shame at their superiority over yourself, or lest you be deceived and puffed up with spiritual pride by the idea that you are better than they. All you need to know is *how much they make of God.* What place, if any, does He occupy in their lives? Thus you will perceive at once whether or not they have the life of God. When we look thus into the lives of very many people we find them almost entirely destitute of the divine element. *God is not in all of their thoughts;* they are practically *god-less,* "*without God.*"

Now how radically and materially different is the life of one who sees God in everything, who refers all things to Him, who receives all things as from Him, and who admits no second causes, but recognizes only the First great Cause, like Job, who referred even the works of the devil to God, for he says,

> *Shall we receive good at the hand of God, and shall we not receive evil?* (Job 2:10).

It was Satan who was bringing evil on Job. Yet the old patriarch refuses to recognize him, but attributes it all (and rightly, too) to God. So "*the man of God*" **consciously** lives and moves and has his being in Him. He lives in his measure "*the life of God*" – that is to say, he lives after God's style.

WHAT IS LIFE?

Perhaps the greatest mystery that presents itself to us in this world of mystery is the mystery of life. What is life? What is it in its essence? We do not know. All we know about it is its phenomena, its outward manifestations. What it is in itself is utterly unknown to us. Hence, when we talk about different kinds of life, what we really mean is different kinds of *living*. Of life in itself of any kind we know nothing, but in the *manner* of life we recognize great differences.

In such cases of the use of the term "life" we are not referring to different kinds of *life* considered in its essence, but to different manners or styles of *living*. The Bible uses the word in the same way. For example, Jesus said,

> Take heed, and beware of covetousness; for a man's
> life consists not in the abundance of the things which
> he possesses (Luke 12:15).

Again He says,

> Take no thought for your life, what you shall eat,
> neither for the body, what you shall put on; the life
> is more than meat, and the body is more than the
> raiment (Matthew 6:25).

Our Lord is not here speaking of life in itself, bare existence, but of a person's *manner* or style of living. Now, when I speak of possessing the life of God, I mean that in some slight degree the believer may live after God's style. He may in a measure have His peace; he may avail himself of God's unchangeableness; he may by faith make God's omnipotence his own (Mark 10:27 with 9:23) and, so hiding under the shadow of the Almighty, he may become a child of the Highest (Luke 6:35) in all kindness, mercy, forbearance and love. In a word, he may view all things from God's standpoint, instead of from man's, and so in a measure live the life of God.

We may come into such close relationship to Him as that our life in a great measure will run along in harmony with His. We shall live with God. His manner of life will be ours; His standpoint will be ours; His thoughts and feelings will be ours. We may even say that His attributes will be ours; His peace, His power, His wisdom, His goodness, *Himself* will be ours. Our life will blend with His and His life will become ours.

> *... For all things are yours; whether Paul, or Apollos, or Cephas, or the world, or life, or death, or things present, or things to come; all are yours; and you are Christ's; and Christ is God's* (I Corinthians 3:21-23).

All this, of course, is not in its perfection, not in its fullness. It is not *"what we shall be"* (I John 3:2) that *"does not yet appear,"* and yet it is a real experience, a positive fact, that life of God begun here and now, although in the perfect and fullest sense we are not made alive unto *"His coming"* (I Corinthians 15:23).

THE GOAL OF ALL CREATION

Surely the advanced Christian is conscious of such a life begun in him, *"in the inward man,"* and it is being *"renewed day by day"* (II Corinthians 4:16). It is a secret, a hidden life that makes him totally different from the natural man. **Everything looks different to him** from what it does to the one who is destitute of this life. The interpretation that he would put on events and the conclusions he would draw therefrom are entirely different, and, in fact, oftentimes directly opposite to the worldly man's interpretations and conclusions.

Where the latter sees chance, or wicked men, or perhaps the devil, the former sees only God. Where the latter man feels fretted, perplexed, angry, indignant, rebellious, the former finds reason for praise, gratitude and thanksgiving. To him *"all things are of God"* (II Corinthians 5:18); hence *all things* are good, and will result in good. There is nothing that can possibly take place in all of the wide circle of the universe that shall not in the end redound to God's honor and glory, and the highest welfare of all His creatures.

Now mark! All of this is part and parcel of the creative process, bringing the creature to the life of the Creator, which is the end of all creation. There is no pleasure in lifeless things or things non-intelligent except as they contribute in some way to the enjoyment and development of *life*. Hence I repeat, *life* or *"the life of God"* is to the end of all creation.

We see also in this view how all things contribute to the perfection of creation, and how all things are so needful to that end. *Everything* gives God occasion and opportunity to reveal Himself to man. For this purpose *nothing* comes amiss. *All things* to this end can be utilized, the evil as well as the good. The Bible is full of illustrations of this truth, that is, how God reveals Himself to man by means of *all things*, and, on the natural plane, especially by evil things.

For this purpose He manifested His power and wrath on Pharaoh and the Egyptians (Exodus 7:5, 17; 14:4, 18), hardening his heart that he should not let the people go, that He might work all His pleasure on that devoted people,

> ... *To the end you may know that I am the Lord* (Exodus 8:22).

> *For the Scripture said to Pharaoh, "Even for this same purpose have I raised you up, that I might show My power in you, and that My name might be declared throughout all the earth"* (Romans 9:17).

> *Nay but, O man, who are you who replies against God? Shall the thing formed say to him who formed*

it, *"Why have You made me thus?" Has not the potter power over the clay, of the same lump to make
one vessel to honor, and another to dishonor?* (Romans 9:20-21).

Here again is a very striking illustration of how *"all things
are of God."* He is the Potter; man is the clay in His hands
(Isaiah 64:8). Also we see how,

> *He works all things after the counsel of His Own will*
> (Ephesians 1:11), and,

> *He does according to His will in the army of heaven,
> and among the inhabitants of the earth: and none
> can stay His hand, or say to Him, "What are You
> doing?"* (Daniel 4:35).

This case also illustrates how God controls and makes
use of evil, and for what purpose. Surely this whole matter of Israel's slavery in Egypt was a great evil, and their
haughty taskmasters were exceedingly wicked in their
cruelty and injustice, and the king endorsed it all, and he
and his subjects were justly punished. Yet the whole thing
was *"of God."*

Centuries before, God had foretold that His people would
go down into Egypt and be afflicted for four hundred
years (Genesis 15:13). When the time came, God sent
them down there (Genesis 46:3). It was God also Who
turned the hearts of the Egyptians to hate His people and
to deal deceitfully with them (Psalms 105:25). He it was
Who hardened Pharaoh's heart that he should not let
them go until He had wrought out all of His mighty judgments on them. Eleven times in this account it said that

God hardened Pharaoh's heart. Paul makes the general statement,

> *Therefore has He mercy on whom He will have mercy, and whom He will He hardens* (Romans 9:18).

The apparent injustice of this entirely disappears in the light of the divine plan of the ages. From the standpoint of orthodoxy the account cannot be reconciled with justice, equity and righteousness, but in the light of the Bible teaching of the redemptive work of the promised Seed in the future ages, all may be adjusted and readily explained, as the intelligent and thoughtful reader will doubtless perceive.

Finally, the purpose of all of this was that *"all the people of the earth might know the hand of the Lord"* (Joshua 4:24). It was an occasion especially prepared beforehand (*"for this same purpose have I raised you up"*) *to the end* that God might reveal Himself, in certain aspects of His character, to man. If the reader will follow out this thought throughout the Bible, he will be surprised, if he has not studied it before, at the amount of Scripture bearing this truth.

Thus God reveals Himself in *all things*, making Himself known. Thus to know God is *life,* and life is the end purpose, the goal of all creation. Hence *all things* contribute to the creation of man. *All things* tend to bring us to God's image and likeness. If *all things* make God known, as they certainly do, since He is in *all things*, then *all things* tend to life, since to know God is life, and this is the consummation of all creation. Thus, we arrive at the true idea of creation, and are able to perceive its process through the natural as well as the spiritual.

GOD'S ORIGINAL PLAN
WILL BE CARRIED OUT

Thus, moreover, we may perceive how certain it is that the original plan of God, which has never been altered or disarranged in the least degree, will be carried out. It is because Christians fail to see that God is not yet finished with man, and that everything around him is part and parcel of the creative process, that they practically make his salvation depend on himself. According to the common idea, God started everything all right. It was by the sin of man that everything was made all wrong, and it is a great mercy on the part of God, entirely unmerited by man, that He has made any provision at all whereby even a *portion* of the race may be saved. If our theology is based on such an error as this, it is no wonder it is still further made ineffective by the idea that man's salvation depends on himself.

Yet we have seen how false and misleading this idea is. We are God's workmanship. We are God's husbandry, God's building, clay in the hands of the Potter – that is, so far as the final accomplishment of the purpose of God is concerned. *"I am the First, and I am the Last,"* says the Lord, and all of this is the creative process.

If Christians could only see this, they would never think of such a thing as making man's perfection depend on himself, for surely in His creative work God needs no assistance. If man's salvation is a new creation, the consummation of which is life, then surely it must be all of God, and *every* son and daughter of the race may rest assured that God's purpose in them individually will be ultimately accomplished. God's offspring (Acts 17:28 compared with

Psalm 82:6) may be absolutely sure that their Father and their Creator will eventually bring them into harmony with Himself. For it is impossible to believe that any portion of His creation will be out of harmony or at variance with Him through all eternity. Especially so, since He plainly declares that He will ultimately *"reconcile all things to Himself"* (Colossians 1:20).

God has a definite purpose in the creation of everything, a definite end in view, and that end is certain to be reached sooner or later. In other words, every creature ultimately fulfills the purpose of the Creator in its creation. For us to suppose otherwise would be to suppose a failure on the part of the Creator, which is unthinkable.

GOD'S PLAN IN ME

The believer's attitude toward God then might be thus expressed: God has created me for a definite purpose. That purpose I shall ultimately fulfill in His economy. It is a wise and good purpose, one with which I should be perfectly satisfied and contented, if I only understood it all. Toward that end I am continually moving. *All things* tend to advance me in that one direction, and I shall surely arrive. I shall surely fulfill the purpose of my creation, and all I have to do is to leave myself in His hands as clay in the hands of the Potter to be fashioned according to His will.

It is a great satisfaction and pleasure to think of our relationship to God in this light, for God has something in His mind to make of me, and I shall surely become that something. Furthermore, since God is wise and good, that something will please and satisfy me perfectly. When

I reach the place for which God created me, and for which
He has fitted me, then I shall have no regrets that it is not
another place, but I shall realize that it is my place and
shall be satisfied, perfectly satisfied with the accomplishment of the ever blessed and good will of God in me.

I am a seed, destined to a certain result ultimately. The
seed may pass through many unexpected changes in
reaching that result, like the seed in the hand of an Egyptian mummy lying dormant for a thousand years, but still
its end is fixed, and that end it will reach, and none other.
I may frustrate the *grace* of God, as in Galatians 2:21, but
I cannot frustrate His *will*. I may be disappointed many
times in failing to be what I would *like* to be, and what
I *imagine* I might have been, and so my *experience* will
correspond to the poet's words,

> Of all sad words by tongue or pen,
> The saddest are these – It might have been.

This *experience* is a part of my training, and by it I am
continually being advanced toward what in the providence of God *I am to be.* Thus,

> *Our place is kept, and it will wait,*
> *Ready for us to fill it, soon or late.*

Let no one say, "This is fatalism." Nay, it is "Godism" if I
may reverently use such an expression. None need fear a
"fatalism" that makes God supreme, absolute, almighty.

In the foregoing remarks I am dealing with finalities. God
is the First and the Last, and He has His way ultimately.
He is *able* to subdue, that is to harmonize, all things to

Himself (Philippians 3:21). He Himself is love, and love has only one way of subduing: by harmonizing. This glorious consummation will be reached when *all are gathered together in one* (Ephesians 1:10) and God is *"All in all"* (I Corinthians 15:28).

Thus may the trusting child *rest in God* both for himself and for the *"whole creation"* (Romans 8:22), and with the utmost confidence that he may commit all of his interests to Him *"as to a faithful Creator"* (I Peter 4:19).

Chapter 2

The Purpose of Evil

I form light and create darkness; I make peace and create evil. I, the Lord, do all these things.

~ Isaiah 45:7

There is probably no subject in all of the range of religious thought so hard to deal with as that of the purpose of evil.

The great question for theologians to wrestle with is this: How can you account for the existence of evil alongside a supreme, all-wise, holy and benevolent God?

Think for a moment on the condition of things in this world. Evil exists on the earth to embitter and darken, to blight and curse everything else that exists. On it goes, rolling through the world, crushing its helpless victims on every hand, and (the saddest feature of all) crushing without distinction the innocent and guilty together in one common quagmire of sin, suffering and death; and God allows it to go on when He might at any instant stop it, and on it has gone for six thousand years.

First let me say that there is no help out of this trouble in orthodoxy. In regard to this subject of orthodoxy [*i.e.*, the doctrine of religion] is hopelessly contradictory and utterly absurd.

Thus orthodoxy speaks: "It was not in God's original plan that evil should exist, but evil has come into existence and done incalculable harm; yet God's plans cannot be thwarted nor disarranged in the least, because He is allwise and almighty. Evil being in existence before man was created, God allows it to come into contact with the man He created when He might have prevented it, knowing full well what the result would be; yet He is in no wise responsible for the consequences of evil. In fact, it is blasphemy to entertain any such idea. Evil having come into existence contrary to God's will, He cannot put it out of existence, but it will continue as long as He exists, an eternal blot on His otherwise perfect universe and a perpetual offense unto all the purified; yet His will is absolute and sovereign and the redeemed will be perfectly happy. Thus, God is in no wise responsible for either the origin, existence, consequences or continuance of evil; yet He can have everything as He pleases, and is the Creator of all things."

So Orthodoxy goes on, stultifying common sense, throttling human reason, and stupidly expecting that intelligent, thoughtful men and women will accept its idiotic patter as the infallible utterances of divine inspiration.

Cannot everyone see that the entire orthodox view is contradictory and absurd in the extreme, and hence self-destructive and untenable?

Now, I hold that the following proposition is self-evident: Given a God of infinite power, wisdom and goodness, He is responsible for ALL things that exist. This also follows from the wisdom and goodness of God: all things that exist are for an intelligent and benevolent end.

These conclusions are inevitable from the premises; they cannot be modified except by modifying the premises. For instance, if you say that some things exist contrary to God's will, then it follows that God is not all-powerful; and you cannot escape this conclusion by bringing in the orthodox doctrine of man's free moral agency, for whatever a free moral agent may do, He is responsible for it who made him a free moral agent. If God made man a free moral agent, He knew beforehand what the result would be, and hence is just as responsible for the consequences of the acts of that free moral agent as He would be for the act of an irresponsible machine that He had made.

Man's free moral agency (free will), even if it was true, would by no means clear God from the responsibility of His acts, since God is his Creator and has made him in the first place just what he is, well knowing what the result would be.

If God's will is EVER thwarted, then He is not almighty. If His will is thwarted, then His plans must be changed, and hence He is not all-wise and immutable. If His will is NEVER thwarted, then all things are in *accordance* with His will and He is responsible for all things as they exist. If He is all-wise and all-good, then all things, existing according to His will, must be tending to some wise and benevolent end.

Thus we come back to my proposition again: If God is infinite in power, wisdom and goodness, then He is responsible for ALL things that exist, and all existing things are tending toward some wise and good end.

He who sees the truth of this proposition will also see the truth of several corollaries depending on it; viz., ABSOLUTE evil cannot exist because God is absolutely GOOD.

The absolute is the unconditioned and unlimited. If there was absolute evil, then the good *would* be limited, and hence *not* absolute, and hence again God would not be absolutely or infinitely good. Yet God IS infinite in goodness, hence evil is NOT infinite. Therefore it is relative, temporary and limited, and therefore again *endless* evil is an impossibility unless you make God less than infinite. Thus it is seen that the doctrine of endless torments is as contrary to reason as it is to Scripture.

We have then arrived purely by reasoning to the somewhat startling and yet perfectly scriptural conclusion that *"all things are of God,"* or God is in all things, or is responsible for all things, including all so-called "evil" things as well as "good" things.

Is not such a position as this very dangerous? Is it not a fearful thing to say that *"evil"* is of God?

I answer that there is nothing dangerous or fearful about this view unless the *truth* is dangerous and fearful. We have seen that reason compels us to this position whether we will or not, and *everyone* familiar with the Bible ought to know that this view is positively Scriptural – that, indeed,

All things are of God (II Corinthians 5:18).

This principle is declared over and over again in the Bible. The prophet Amos goes so far as to particularize evil as "of God" when in his question he makes an implied statement which, from an orthodox standpoint, would be blasphemous:

> *Shall there be evil in a city, and the Lord has not done it?* (Amos 3:6).

Thus Job similarly asks,

> *What? Shall we receive good at the hand of God, and shall we not receive evil?* (Job 2:10).

What is still more to the purpose, we have the direct positive statement that GOD *creates evil!*

> *I form light and create darkness; I make peace and create evil. I, the Lord, do all these things* (Isaiah 45:7).

This passage is most strange and unaccountable on the ground of any of the current orthodox creeds. God creates evil? It cannot be! Yet here it is in the Word. What will you do with it? "We must explain it somehow," says Orthodoxy, "and yet save our creed."

How shall it be done? Orthodoxy shall answer, "Suppose we say that the evil here spoken of is not moral evil, sin or wrongdoing, but physical evil, famines, pestilences, tornadoes, etc., which God controls and sends on mankind as punishment for their wickedness."

That will not do! The word here rendered evil is the one

commonly used throughout the Old Testament to denote wickedness, sin, wrongdoing. In some five hundred passages it is so used.[1] The very same Greek word is also rendered "wicked" and "wickedness" more than a hundred times.[2]

Suppose that, instead of trying to explain this passage in harmony with some cut-and-dried creed, we let all creeds go and see if we can find out what the passage really means, and then, if the creed does not harmonize with that meaning, throw the creed away and form another one that will harmonize with it.

At any rate, here is the statement in the Word and we will be brave enough to receive it as truth and trust the same One who made it to explain it. Since God is infinitely good and wise, and evil is one of His creatures, it must be that evil shall finally result in some good and wise end, as we have already seen.

How can that be? If we can by any means understand how it can be, the next question would be, What can it be? What can be the end, good and wise, toward which evil is tending?

We can understand how all evil ultimately tends to good from the fact that we know from our own experience how some evil tends to good, and in the Bible and in the world around us we see the same thing illustrated again and again.

As for you, ye thought evil against me; but God

1. For example, see Genesis 6:5; Numbers 14:27; Deuteronomy 31:29; I Kings 11:6; 16:30; Psalms 34:21.
2. See for example Genesis 6:5; 13:13; Psalm. 94:23; 101:4.

meant it unto good (Genesis 50:20).

Now if God has done this in some cases, and if, as we know, He *"works all things after the counsel of His Own will"* (Ephesians 1:11), then surely it is not difficult to believe that He overrules all evil for good.

In fact, this must be so, for it is only on this ground, *i.e.*, that all evil ultimately tends to good in the end, that we can harmonize the existence of evil at all with the existence of a God of infinite power, wisdom and love.

It is not necessary for us to understand how in each particular case evil is overruled for good in order to believe that it is so overruled. The subject is made still clearer, moreover, from the fact that we can see and understand what some of these good ends are toward which evil conducts us, and thus we come to know something of the purpose of evil.

We see furthermore that this purpose is grand and glorious and in perfect harmony with the character of God and that it fully accounts for the existence of evil.

For example, how could God ever reveal Himself to man in His mercy, long-suffering and compassion if it had not been that evil had put us into a position to call for the exercise of these attributes in our behalf? Furthermore, especially how could God manifest to us His love in all of its intensity and greatness except by such an opportunity as evil furnishes? As it is written,

> *In this was manifested the love of God toward us, because God sent His only Son into the world that*

we might live through Him (I John 4:9).

There could have been no such manifestation of the Father's love if there had been no such thing as evil.

We might believe that a friend loved us even though his love had never been especially tested, but we never could appreciate his love unless circumstances transpired to give him an opportunity to exhibit it in all of its strength and fullness.

So, too, we never could understand fully the love of God (and hence never could know Him fully, I Corinthians 13:12, for *"God is love"*) had it not been for our lost and wretched condition furnishing the Father with an adequate opportunity for its manifestation. It was *"when we were yet without strength"* (Romans 5:6) that Christ died for us.

> *God commendeth His love toward us in that while we were yet sinners Christ died for us* (Romans 5:8).

It was because we were in such an evil case, without strength and sinners, that the love that sent the Deliverer is so marked and readily appreciated. Hence,

> *Hereby perceive we the love of God, because He* [Christ] *laid down His life for us* (I John 3:16).

How should we have been able thus to perceive that love in its so great plenitude if we had never come under the power of evil so as to need this extreme manifestation of it?

Furthermore, as evil gives God an occasion to reveal Himself to us so that we may know Him, so it gives us the opportunity to exercise the attributes of God so that we may become like Him.

The existence of evil in the world gives the child of God the opportunity for the exercise of the godlike attributes of mercy, compassion, forgiveness, forbearance, meekness, and gentleness and thus he becomes like God;

> *for He makes His sun to rise on the evil and on the good, and sends rain on the just and on the unjust ... He is kind to the unthankful and to the evil"* (Matthew 5:45; Luke 6:35).

Thus we see something of the purpose of evil in the blessings of mankind.

In addition to all of this, we have other direct testimony from Scripture that evil is one of God's ministers for ultimate good. It is clearly intimated again and again that God uses evil for the accomplishment of His plans which, of course, are always good.

> *For I reckon that the sufferings of this present time are not worthy to be compared with the glory which shall be revealed in us* (Romans 8:18).

See, for instance, Judges 9:23. Read the context and you will see that Abimelech by a most atrocious crime had obtained the rulership of Israel, and to punish him,

> *God sent an evil spirit between him and the men of Schechem.*

The result was the punishment of all of the guilty parties.

See the same idea in I Samuel 16:14.

> *The Spirit of the Lord departed from Saul and an evil spirit from the Lord troubled him.*

This evil spirit did not come from the devil nor from hell, but *from the Lord* to do His bidding.

See also I Kings 22:23 where the Lord is represented as using a *"lying spirit"* in order to deceive wicked Ahab for his own destruction.

The case of Job is one of the most striking and perfect illustrations of this wonderful truth. The Lord speaks of him as,

> *My servant Job, that there is none like him in the earth, a perfect and an upright man, one who fears God, and eschews evil* (Job 1:8).

Thus it appears that Job was a remarkably good man, and this is confirmed by Ezekiel 14:14, 20.

> *"Though these three men, Noah, Daniel, and Job, were in it, they should deliver but their own souls by their righteousness," says the Lord God ... "Though Noah, Daniel, and Job, were in it, as I live," says the Lord GOD, "they shall deliver neither son nor daughter; they shall but deliver their own souls by their righteousness."*

Now then, what does God do but deliberately hand over this perfect and upright man into the hands of Satan to do his worst to him, only that he should not touch his life.

How could we have a more perfect illustration of how God uses evil as an instrument for good? Although Job suffered intensely, we know that in the end he was greatly blessed by his hard and bitter experience.

If God thus uses Satan, the embodiment of evil, as a minister for ultimate good in the case of one individual, is it hard to believe that all evil is overruled of God for good in all cases?

The New Testament teaches the same truth. Did you ever notice how strangely the evangelists Matthew and Mark speak of Christ's temptation? The Spirit drove Jesus into the wilderness to be tempted of the devil (Matthew 4:1; Mark 1:12-13). What a strange statement! The Holy Spirit of God drives the sinless Jesus into the wilderness to be tempted of Satan, the arch enemy of all good, a murderer from the beginning, and the father of lies!

Truly God creates evil and uses it, too, for His Own purposes and glory! The apostle Paul fully understood this great truth and practiced it himself. Hence he writes to the Corinthians,

> *To deliver such a one to Satan for the destruction of the flesh that the spirit may be saved in the day of the Lord Jesus* (I Corinthians 5:5).

He declares in his letter to Timothy that he himself had delivered certain ones to Satan,

> *That they might learn not to blaspheme* (I Timothy 1:20).

It would seem also that the apostle knew something of this kind of discipline himself, for he says,

> *Lest I should be exalted above measure through the abundance of the revelations, there was given me a thorn in the flesh, the messenger of Satan to buffet me, lest I should be exalted above measure* (II Corinthians 12:7).

All of this clearly proves that God overrules evil for good, and that even Satan's work ultimately shall result in blessings for God's children.

Finally, we will notice one other passage more remarkable, if possible, even than those I have cited.

In the 20th chapter of the Revelation we have an account of the total restraint of the devil and consequent suppression of evil for a thousand years. What a blessed era of peace and righteousness that will be, and how desirable that it should continue and that evil should never again curse the earth!

Then at the end of the thousand years Satan is loosed out of his prison, and again goes out to deceive the nations, and peace is banished from the earth, and war and slaughter ensues with terrible suffering and destruction. According to the orthodox idea of the origin and final effects of evil, there would seem to be some terrible mistake here. Either Satan is not watched closely enough, or his prison was insecure, or there was treachery; some awful blunder or more awful crime has been committed to let the devil loose when once he was well secured, surely it would seem from the orthodox standpoint. Yet, so it is not.

All is plain when we see the great truth I have tried to set forth. Satan is God's servant to carry out His plans. He is just as much under God's control and works; just as truly under His direction as is Gabriel. God now leaves him free to work out his mischievous will among the children of men. Satan is the,

Prince of this world (John 12:31; 14:30; 16:11);

The spirit that works in the children of disobedience (Ephesians 2:2).

The time will come when he will be bound and put under total restraint and so remain through the Millennium. Then he will be loosed because God has something more for him to do, and he will finally be disposed, but we have seen that evil is needful and beneficial in the end. It is one of God's creatures and His servant, and is conducive to the accomplishment of His gracious plans, as are all other things.

Thus the Word untangles this great mystery of evil for us and shows us clearly that it is not an interloper in God's economy. It is not a foreign substance in the delicate fabric of God's great plan, obstructing and disarranging its intricate mechanism; nay, it is a necessary part of that plan.

It rightly belongs to the marvelous congeries [stockpiles] of forces, that under the control and guidance of the One Supreme mind, works and interworks steadily and without interruption or delay to the glorious end of creating a divine and god-like race. Thank God that on this, as in all other things, He will be glorified and man, in the end, be blessed!

Now, another thought. There are some who say that they could accept the foregoing position if it was not for one thing: the great injustice that there is in the world. They can see how God can overrule evil for good in the case of the guilty. Those who deserve punishment are benefited by it, but the evil of this world falls with equal weight on the innocent as on the guilty, and even in many cases with greater weight on the former than on the latter.

The sins of the fathers are visited on the children. The innocent and helpless suffer most keenly on account of the viciousness and brutality of others, and thus the most outrageous injustice is perpetrated continually around us in the world.

How can all of this be permitted in the dominions of a God of absolute justice and boundless love? How can all of this be conducive to good? Is there an answer to this tremendous problem? Two considerations, if I err not, will help us to a solution.

We have seen that one of the purposes of evil is to develop in our character attributes from God: pity, mercy, compassion, charity, gentleness, etc. Now suppose we lived in a world of absolute justice where no one suffered except what they strictly deserved to suffer, where the innocent never suffered, but only the guilty, and they suffered just so much – no more and no less – as was due to their transgression and as would be beneficial to the transgressor.

Suppose we lived in such a world as that. At first thought it would seem as though it would be a very nice kind of world; but how could we in such a world develop the god-like attributes above referred to?

There would be no room for heavenly compassion and sweet charity and pity in a world of absolute justice. We would not be likely to pity very much a person who we knew was receiving only the punishment due his fault and that in the end would be for his benefit and blessing.

Is it not plain that just this kind of evil, *i.e.*, the evil of injustice, is needed in order that those crowning attributes of God, the tender and loving qualities of our Father in heaven, may be developed and perfected in His human children?

Furthermore, so far as the injustice goes, that may be only temporary and apparent. Who shall say that in future cycles which God's plan has yet to run, all of the apparent injustice of this present time may not be perfectly adjusted, taken into account, and made right? Surely no one has any right to say that it will not be so; and it is perfectly reasonable and probable that it will be so.

Yet there is still another consideration that fully confirms all of the foregoing and still further explains the whole subject. We should always endeavor to discover the underlying principles of God's actions. Nothing that God does is arbitrary or capricious, but every one of His movements has an adequate and righteous cause. He always acts from principle. The outward act may change under different circumstances and toward different individuals, but His principles of action never change.

See this whole subject set forth in Ezekiel, chapter forty three. Hence, in order to become acquainted with God, to know Him more and more, we must endeavor to understand, not simply what God does, but why He does it.

To know merely what God does is often times very puzzling and inexplicable. To know why He does it makes all as clear and luminous as noon day. What we need to know, then, in order to know God, are the reasons for God's actions – the purpose, *"the end of the Lord"* (James 5:11), the causes and principles of His movements and operations in His dealings with mankind. We may always be sure that there is a just and righteous reason for all of God's ways and our endeavor should be to know and understand that reason.

Now let us apply this to the subject we are considering. Evil exists, things that seem utterly antagonistic to God and His way, but which we are sure from the foregoing considerations to be, in some sense of God, in harmony with His will, and conducive to the furtherance of His plans.

Now then, is there any principle of action, just and righteous in itself, that will account for the existence of evil and indicate its ultimate result?

There certainly is such a principle, thus: It is a recognized principle in law and equity that it is right and just to inflict or permit temporary evil for the sake of an ultimate and permanent good. This principle, all will see, is certainly correct.

It is on this principle that all punishment of any kind is justifiable, and it is only on this principle that it can be justified. Punishment is an evil, but it is an evil that may finally result in good, and when it is inflicted for such a purpose, it is right and just.

Now we know from numerous examples, many of which I have given, that God acts on this principle. He uses evil as an ultimate instrument for good. Admit that this principle is correct and that God acts on it, and all is at once accounted for and its final result indicated.

This sweeping conclusion may not at once be clear to all, but a little thought will show that it is fully justified. If it is right to use evil as an ultimate instrument for good, and if God acts on this principle, the principle fully explaining and justifying the act, then is it not reasonable to conclude that all evil is so justified?

We cannot enter sufficiently deep into God's plans to be able to explain the how and the why of each individual case; but, once admitting the principle, and seeing numerous examples of its application that we can understand, the conclusion is fully warranted that this principle applies to all cases.

Of course, no one could accept this conclusion who believed in endless torment. The above principle will not explain or justify unmitigated and eternal evil. I have already shown that such evil really dethrones God, or at least shares His throne with Him, which is equivalent to dethroning Him. To say that evil is absolute and eternal is to fully invest it with attributes peculiar to Deity; but this cannot be. At that rate there would be two gods – a good and a bad one – and each of them would exist eternally and be eternal foes. To such a frightful conclusion does the doctrine of the eternity of evil lead us. Let those believe it who can; but if we take the Bible teaching on this subject, the principle enunciated fully accounts for and explains the existence and purpose of evil.

It may seem to some that this principle cannot apply to all evil. They are able to see how some evil may be overruled for good, but that all the terrible forms of evil can be so overruled seems to them impossible. Yet such a question is simply one of degree.

If God can make some evil conducive to good, can He not so make all evil of whatever form or quantity? If it is true that God uses evil for good at all, how can we tell, not knowing perfectly God's plans and methods, just what kind of evil and just how much evil God will so use?

We must conclude that all of the evil we see about us in every horrifying form and in all of its vast amount comes under the same category of part and parcel of the great plan that through sin, corruption, chaos and death is moving on to holiness, purity, order and life eternal.

> *Moreover the law entered, that the offense might abound. But where sin abounded, grace did much more abound* (Romans 5:20).

Furthermore, the final outcome of God's plan, so clearly revealed in Scripture, fully confirms the foregoing view and, in fact, irresistibly drives us to that view.

All of the details and every particular of the plan in all of its length and breadth are not revealed, but the result is revealed. That result, the final outcome, is a perfect and absolute triumph for goodness, truth and justice.

> *Every knee shall bow ... and every tongue shall confess ... to the glory*[3] *of God* (Philippians 2:10-11; Romans 14:11; Isaiah 45:23).

---

3. Also translated in other places as *"praise"* and *"worship."*

The creature ... shall be delivered from the bondage of corruption (Romans 8:21).

That ... He might gather together in one all things in Christ (Ephesians 1:10).

Then shall be brought to pass the saying that is written, "Death is swallowed up in victory" (I Corinthians 15:54).

There shall be no more curse (Revelation 22:3).

The people which shall be created shall praise the Lord (Psalms 102:18).

This is the outcome! Thank God, it is good enough! To this final result all things are tending. To such a universal victory we are traveling on. We can see it by faith afar off.

> I cannot doubt that good shall fall
> At last, far off, at last to all.

Thus does reason and the Word set forth the purpose of evil. My feeble powers of expression are altogether inadequate for the full presentation of the great truth, but these thoughts will suggest the solution to the problem and will help the lover of truth to a deeper and fuller apprehension of the unique and wonderful ways of God;

Lo, these are parts of His ways; but how little a portion is heard of Him? But the thunder of His power, who can understand? (Job 26:14).

II Corinthians 12 : 9
My grace is sufficient
for you, for My strength
is made perfect in weakness.
(12:10) Therefore, most gladly I will
rather boast in my infirmities,
in reproaches, in needs,
in persecutions, in distress for
Christ's sake. For when I am
weak, then I am strong.

Chapter 3

The Purpose of Trials

I am exceeding joyful in all our tribulation.
~ II Corinthians 7:4

I glory... in mine infirmities.
~ II Corinthians 12:5

... We glory in tribulations also ...
~ Romans 5:3

*P*aul said, *"We glory in tribulation also."* How is it possible to have such an experience?

Every true Christian knows something of being resigned in tribulations. It is thought to be a great triumph of grace if, in the midst of troubles, distress and persecutions one is uncomplaining, submissive and patient.

Yet to *"glory in tribulations," "to take pleasure in infirmities, in reproaches, in necessities, in persecutions, in distresses"* (II Corinthians 12:10), to actually take pleasure in such things, this is an experience that very few know anything about; indeed to most it seems an impossible experience; it seems moreover utterly unreasonable to expect any such thing.

How can a person take pleasure in that which is unpleas-
ant and painful? The thing is contrary to nature, and
indeed seems contrary to common sense; and yet what
shall we do with the numerous Scriptures that plainly set
forth this experience, like those I have quoted above, and
many others to the same effect?

Such an experience must be possible, for Paul and Peter
and the other apostles and early Christians had it, and
speak of it in the Bible as a thing within.

I apprehend that the reason why so few understand this
experience is because they read the Word so carelessly,
and understand so little about God's way of life. *"Made
perfect through suffering"* (Hebrews 2:10), and *"through
death to life"* (Romans 4:25), is God's way, and the one
secret of *"glorying in tribulations,"* is to understand **the
purpose of trials**.

KEEPING ONE'S EYES ON THE RESULT

He who has his *eye* on the result, when that result is grand
and glorious beyond all expression or comparison, will
reckon little of the means, especially if he realizes that
they are the *only* possible means, and at the same time
the absolutely *certain* means to reach the desired end.

Herein lies the whole secret of this wonderful experience; a worldly person might glory in the severest trials and sufferings if they were absolutely sure that they
would thereby reach some lofty position of honor, power and wealth; he would not glory in the sufferings for
their own sake, but for the sake of the final outcome.

So the Christian can *"glory in tribulations,"* and *"take pleasure in distresses,"* if he knows that thereby he is drawing nearer and nearer to the life of God. This is just what the Scriptures teach; now we will look at a few passages.

Paul says,

> *We glory in tribulations, **knowing** that tribulation works patience; and patience, experience; and experience, hope; and hope makes not ashamed, because the love of God is shed abroad in our hearts by the Holy Spirit which is given to us* (Romans 5:3-5).

The whole point in this passage depends on seeing the force of the word *"knowing."* We glory in tribulations, ***"knowing** that tribulation works patience,"* etc.

Do *you* know this? Do you *know* that our troubles and sorrows and distresses refine and sanctify us, and make us *"meet for the inheritance of the saints in light"* (Colossians 1:12)?

Do you know that this is the *only* way whereby we may be made thus meet? Do you desire a seat with Christ on His throne? A share in His reign?

Our trials are the means whereby we are fitted for the place God has for us in His kingdom. They give us the necessary training for our office in that kingdom; hence they are the price we have to pay for a government position under the Lord Jesus Christ.

It is the knowledge of this fact, *viz.,* that every trial properly borne brings us nearer to perfection and the reward, which enables the believer not only to bear them with patience and resignation, but even to rejoice in them, since we know that though

> For the present they are not joyous but grievous, yet afterward they yield the peaceable fruits of righteousness (Hebrews 12:11).

Our God is a reasonable Being. He says, *"Come now, let us reason together"* (Isaiah 1:18). He deals with us on common sense principles. God's ways, when rightly understood, will commend themselves to our own judgment; His requirements and precepts *are just what we should choose ourselves had we the same knowledge.* Hence when we come to understand His ways, we readily conform to them because we see that they are best, that this is our *"reasonable service"* (Romans 12:1).

Now then, in regard to trials, if we can only see and understand that they are needful for our training to fit us for a glorious and blessed future, then although we could not rejoice in the trial for its own sake, we could rejoice in it, yea, we could take pleasure in it, for the sake of the benefit we were to derive therefrom in the end.

Men of the world act on this principle. The Athlete submits to the most rigid training and to great self denial for months together, in order that he may gain the prize in the walking, rowing, or sparring match, or in some other contest of muscle and brawn. *"Now they do it to obtain a corruptible crown; but we an incorruptible"* (I Corinthians 9:19-27).

If God has opened your eyes to see something of the glories

of the coming kingdom, if the veil of sense has been removed that you have caught a glimpse of the things beyond, *"the unseen things"* (II Corinthians 4:18) you will understand that the path to those glories lies through trial, suffering and affliction that you may reap the reward by and by.

The apostle says,

> *Our light afflictions, which are but for a moment work out for us a far more exceeding and eternal weight of glory* (II Corinthians 4:17).

Most people stop here and so lose the whole point of the passage. They say, "My afflictions are not light and momentary; they are heavy and continuous, far beyond that of other people, and I cannot see how they are of any benefit to me, nor how I can rejoice in them." Read the next verse and you will understand how to obtain the experience set forth.

> *Our light afflictions, which are but for a moment, work out for us a far more exceeding and eternal weight of glory,* **while we look not at the things that are seen, but at the things that are not seen;** *for the things that are seen are temporal but the things that are not seen are eternal* (II Corinthians 4:17-18).

WHAT ARE YOU LOOKING AT?

Afflicted brother or sister, what are you looking at? Are you looking at yourself and your trials? Are you looking with envious eyes at your neighbors and friends whom you think have an easier time than you? Are you looking with longing eyes at the pleasures and enjoyments, the apparent peace and comfort of others? Wishing that you might possess the same, and comparing your hard circumstances with their apparently pleasant ones?

While you look at such things as these you will not find your afflictions light and momentary, neither will they work out for you the wonderful glory of which Paul speaks. It is only WHILE you look not at the things that are seen, but at the things that are not seen, not seen by the natural eye but apprehended by the eye of faith (Hebrews 11:13-16), that your afflictions become easily bearable and work out for you the far more exceeding and eternal weight of glory; your afflictions become light and momentary by comparison with the exceeding glory of the unseen and eternal things; as the apostle says again,

> I reckon that the sufferings of this present time are not worthy to be compared with the glory which shall be revealed in us (Romans 8:18).

Not Worthy

Our present sufferings are often times great in themselves, and sometimes they seem overwhelming while we are looking at them, or comparing them with the apparently pleasant circumstances of others, but they *"are not worthy to be compared with the glory which shall be revealed in us."*

So Paul thought when he counted

> all things but loss for the excellency of the knowledge of Christ Jesus my Lord ... that I may know Him, and the power of His resurrection, and the fel-

*lowship of His sufferings, being made conformable
to His death; if by any means I might attain to the
resurrection of the dead* (Philippians 3:8, 10-11).

The ancient worthies were actuated by the same intense
desire, *"not accepting deliverance"* from their cruel persecutions, *"that they might obtain a better resurrection"*
(Hebrews 11:35).

Moses *"chose rather to suffer affliction with the people
of God than to enjoy the pleasures of sin for a season.
Esteeming the reproach of Christ greater riches than the
treasures in Egypt, for he had respect to the recompense
of the reward"* (Hebrews 11:25).

Jesus Christ Himself *"endured the cross, despising the
shame, for the joy that was set before Him"* (Hebrew 12:2).
So, also Jesus taught. Listen! *"Blessed are you when men
shall hate you."*

What! Blessed are you when men shall hate you (Luke
6:22-23)! Is that the way it reads? Yes, that's the way it
reads; but hear the rest:

*Blessed are you when men shall hate you, and when
they shall separate you from their company, and
shall reproach you, and shall say all manner of evil
against you falsely for the Son of man's sake. Rejoice
in that day, and leap for joy, for behold, your reward
is great in heaven; for in like manner did they to the
prophets.*

Well, well, that's a strange *"blessed."* Blessed when we
are hated; we are to rejoice and leap for joy when we are

reproached, and slandered, and cast out; that's too much for *human nature.*

Yes, it is too much for human nature, but it is not too much for the *divine nature,* of which we are made *"partakers"* by the *"exceeding great and precious promises"* (I Peter 4:4).

These promises are God's notes of hand and are good for their full face value, and more, yea, *"much more"* (Romans 5:17), because the Great Promisor is *"able to do exceeding abundantly above all that we ask or think"* (Ephesians 3:20). Yet let two things be remembered in regard to the above quoted words of Jesus, *"and shall say all manner of evil against you falsely for the Son of man's sake"* (Matthew 5:11).

If you are spoken against falsely, and for Christ's sake, then this "Blessed" is yours, and you may rejoice in it. However,

> *What glory is it if, when you are buffeted for your faults, you shall take it patiently? But if, when you do well and suffer for it, you take it patiently, this is acceptable with God. For even hereto were you called, because Christ also suffered for us, leaving us an example, that we should follow His steps* (I Peter 2:20-21).

We sometimes hear persons say when they are suffering from the ill will or unkindness of others, "If I had done anything to merit such treatment I would not say anything; but to be accused falsely, and be ill treated when you are not to blame, is more than I can bear." It is not more than Christ bore, and He *"did no sin, neither was guile found in His mouth"* (I Peter 2:22) and *"if any man has not the spirit of Christ He is none of His"* (Romans 8:9).

OUR CALLING

Sufferings, afflictions, trials, etc., are a part of the believer's *"calling"* in this age.

Whatever calling, profession or occupation a man may choose, he would, of course, expect to pass through a certain process of study, discipline and training to fit him for that calling, and that preparatory process is a necessary part of the calling.

So it is in *"the High Calling of God in Christ Jesus"* (Philippians 3:14).

The process by which we are prepared for the high position is, of course, a part of the calling.

Therefore,

> *Beloved, think it not strange concerning the fiery trial which is to try you, as though some strange thing happened to you,* [rather, take it as a matter of course, an expected part of your training] *and rejoice, inasmuch as you are partakers of Christ's sufferings, that when His glory shall be revealed you may be glad also with exceeding joy; if you are reproached for the name of Christ, happy are you, for the spirit of glory and of God rests on you* (I Peter 4:12-14).
>
> *If we suffer with Him we shall also reign with Him* (II Timothy 2:12).

Thus are we,

> *Heirs of God, and joint heirs with Jesus Christ, if
> so be that we suffer with Him, that we may be also
> glorified together* (Romans 8:17).

You desire to be glorified with Him by-and-by, but are
you unwilling to walk with Him now in the suffering, hu-
miliation and reproach, and thereby *"fill up that which is
behind of the afflictions of Christ"* (Colossians 1:24)?

It is only as we know now something of *"the fellowship of
His sufferings"* (Philippians 3:10) that we shall know by-
and-by, *"the power of His resurrection."* What a wonderful privilege it is thus to be permitted to share with Christ
in His sufferings and His glory!

> *To you it is given in the behalf of Christ, not only to
> believe on Him but also to suffer for His sake* (Philip-
> pians 1: 29).

If we *"see our calling"* (I Corinthians 1:26), we shall *"rejoice that we are counted worthy to suffer shame for the
name of Christ"* (Acts 5: 41).

Therefore,

> *My Brothers, count it all joy when you fall into di-
> verse temptations* [trials], **knowing this,** *that the
> trying of your faith works patience. But let patience
> have its perfect work that you may be perfect and
> entire, wanting nothing* (James 1:2-4).

ALL JOY

Here again the whole force of the passage depends on the word *"knowing."* If you know the truth set forth in the latter part of the passage, you will have no difficulty about the experience of the first part. You can count your trials *"all joy,"* if you only know that thereby you are being continually advanced toward that condition where you will be *"perfect and entire, wanting nothing."*

If you do not know this great truth, the idea of counting trials *"all joy"* will seem impossible and even foolish to you. In other words, if we understand the purpose of trials, we shall not only be resigned to them, but we can glory in them, yea *"take pleasure"* in them, *"in infirmities, reproaches, necessities, persecutions, distresses, for Christ's sake, that the power of Christ may rest on us"* (II Corinthians 12:9).

The hardest trials we have to bear are injustice, misrepresentation, slander, false accusation, but this is just what we need to perfect our patience, and fit us for a place in the coming kingdom. The Lord's jewels need cutting, grinding and polishing before they shall be fit to be set in His *"crown of rejoicing"* (I Thessalonians. 2:19).

The severer the process the more brilliant will be the finished gem, and the more perfectly will it be able to flash forth the reflection of the glories of the great Artificer. Hence the believer, fortified with this knowledge of the purpose of evil, can "smile at the storm," knowing that – let it blow ever so hard and so angry – the gale can only "drive them nearer home."

Perhaps someone is ready to ask at this point "Is not the believer ever to be sad and sorrowful? Should he always be full of joy and mirth no matter what comes?" Surely the child of God is sad and sorrowful oftentimes. Frequently, there is but very little mirth in his heart, and yet he may rejoice even while he weeps. Did you never read Paul's Paradoxes?

> In all things approving ourselves as the ministers of God ... by honor and dishonor, by evil report and good report, as deceivers and yet true, as unknown and yet well known, as dying and behold we live, as chastened and not killed, as sorrowful, yet always rejoicing, as poor yet making many rich, as having nothing and yet possessing all things (II Corinthians 6:4-10).

Oh wonderful and blessed experience of life in death, joy in sorrow, riches in poverty, *"all things"* in *"nothing!"* Foolishness to the natural man, but luminous with glory to him who is spiritual! Yet, alas, how few there are who know anything about this experience. Some *"love this present world"* (II Timothy 4:10) so well that they do not know enough even to be resigned in trials, much less to glory in them.

THE AUDACITY OF FAITH

"When the Son of man comes, shall He find faith on the earth?" (Luke 18:8). There is plenty of the spurious article, but where is the genuine? Oh, that you and I, friend reader, may be among the few who shall possess that clearness of spiritual insight and audacity of faith that shall enable us to *"glory in tribulation,"* to *"take pleasure in*

infirmities," and to *"rejoice and leap for joy"* even on account of those things that the world would reckon among the worst calamities.

"What! shall we receive good at the hand of God, and shall we not receive evil?" (Job 2:10). He is equally the Creator of both, and both shall equally *"work together for good to them who love God"* (Romans 8:28). Therefore, *"O you afflicted, tossed with tempest, and not comforted"* (Isaiah. 54:11) triumph over your trials and afflictions by this knowledge of their purpose, for the Lord has said, *"No I will never leave you; no, no, I will not forsake you"*(Hebrews 13:5).

In a fashionable gathering, a young man who affected infidelity heard that a lady of note, then present, professed to believe the Bible. Finding her out in the company, he made bold to ask if it was true that she believed the Bible. "Yes, sir, I do most certainly," replied the lady decidedly. "Why do you believe it?" still further queried the skeptic. "Because I am acquainted with the Author," was the quick reply, that effectually put a stop to all further questioning.

> *Thus says the Lord, "Let not the wise man glory in his wisdom, neither let the mighty man glory in his might, let not the rich man glory in his riches, but let him who glories glory in this, that he understands and knows ME, that I am the Lord Who exercises loving kindness, judgment and righteousness in the earth; for in these things I delight," says the Lord* (Jeremiah 9:23-24).

Chapter 4

The Purpose of Failure

O Israel, you have destroyed yourself; but in Me is your help.

~ Hosea 13:9

You turn man to destruction; and say, "Return, you children of men."

~ Psalms 90:3

The history of mankind is one of continuous and unvarying "failure." The reason is that the human race as yet is only in the first stage of its development. The regular cycle of man's life includes two stages: first the natural, afterwards the spiritual – two planes.

Howbeit that was not first which is spiritual, but that which is natural; and afterward that which is spiritual (I Corinthians 15:46).

The metamorphosis from the lower to the higher has not yet taken place. God never intended that the physical man should succeed. He must wait until after the change comes. Then he shall have good success.

I do not intend to undertake here to prove the foregoing. I only notice briefly a few points. When I speak above of success, I mean on the higher plane. Man's achievements have been most notable and marvelous, but always on the lower plane.

After the interval of death, whether long or short or instantaneous, the individual picks up the thread of his development and goes on to finish whatever it may be in God's plan precisely as after an interval of natural sleep. As long as one is on the natural plane, his normal, intended advance is one of blundering, hesitation and failure. He is advancing all of the time, but in a very erratic and apparently roundabout way.

God utilizes all things, good and bad, to the furtherance of His plans concerning each individual as well as the whole great macrocosm. Hence failure on the physical plane is man's normal status.

THE FAILURE IN EDEN

This is illustrated in the primal failure through which Eden was lost. Listen!

> And the Lord God said, "Behold, the man is become as one of Us, to know good and evil; and now, lest he puts forth his hand and takes also of the Tree of Life, and eats, and lives forever:" therefore the Lord God sent him forth from the garden of Eden, to till the ground from which he was taken (Genesis 3:22-23).

The insertion of the word "also" shows us that as yet man

had not partaken of the Tree of Life, and God did not intend that he should and so live forever in a state of failure.

So He drove out the man; and He placed at the east of the Garden of Eden Cherubims, and a flaming sword which turned every way, to keep the way of the Tree of Life (Genesis 3:24).

Man must be excluded from the Tree of Life until he is fit to approach and to partake of it; but in the meantime, the way to it must not be lost, and so Cherubim and flaming sword are placed on guard to keep the way for man until at last he shall enter into the life that is life indeed.

The partaking of the Tree of Life is the crowning work of man's creation and, of course, cannot be realized until the second stage of his progress, for first the natural and afterwards that which is spiritual.

I said to a neighbor today, "It's a good thing to be alive." He had just remarked upon the beauty of the day and the pleasure of knowing that warm weather was approaching. I responded to his cheery greeting and made the above remark, to which he replied, somewhat to my surprise, "Well, I don't know. This is a hard world, full of disappointment and sorrow." We had a little talk. I told him that the world was not finished yet. Neither were we, and we would not like to have our world criticized and disparaged before it was complete. Wait until the Maker of all has finished His work; then we would see that all was well done and everyone satisfied.

I don't know how much my neighbor got out of this talk, or whether he got anything at all, but afterwards, speaking of the conversation to my wife, I said, "Probably the reason for him speaking in such a gloomy way is because he has not yet begun to live at all."

> He who has the Son has life: He who has not the Son of God has not life (I John 5:12).

To have the Son is to possess the divine life, as Paul the apostle says,

> I live, yet not I, but Christ lives in me; and the life that I now live in the flesh I live by the faith of the Son of God Who loved me and gave Himself for me (Galatians 2:20).

Christ is our life, and we live it through His faith – "the faith of the Son of God."

> When Christ, **Who is our life,** shall appear, then shall you also appear with Him in glory (Colossians 3:4).

> He who has not this life has no life and knows not the joy of living (John 6:53-57).

THE FAILURE AT THE FLOOD

The next failure after Eden culminated with the flood. Read the first dozen verses of the sixth chapter of Genesis and note what a terrible failure that was – and was it not disgraceful, too? Disgraceful to the Creator, I mean? I once listened to a lecture by a so-called infidel in which he criticized the matter of the flood about as follows. He said that,

According to the Bible, God created man, the first pair; and the first thing they did was to disobey their Maker and get turned out of Eden. Then the first male child that was born became a murderer, a fratricide. Then, as men increased, they grew worse and worse until they became unspeakably wicked and corrupt. So the Creator was sorry that He had made man, the race, and finally He had to drown them all but one family, and begin all over again with that family. But the utter foolishness of the whole procedure is shown by the fact that the race was started again after the flood by a family that was no better than those that had drowned, for the first thing Noah did was to get drunk. During his debauch one of his children grossly insulted him so that, when he became sober, he put a perpetual curse upon Canaan, the son of Ham, and forthwith the world began to grow as bad as ever. This declension culminated at the tower of Babel and was punished by the confusion of the tongues and the dispersion.

Now I do not hesitate to admit frankly that from the lower plane the contention of the infidel is well taken. The whole affair seems to be a sad reflection on the wisdom and power of the Creator, a disgrace to Him and a miserable fizzle; and yet he who understands the mystery of the pneumic (spiritual) can know that there was no failure and no disgrace. It was simply just as God intends, perfectly normal and fully provided for. That which is perfect is not yet come.

THE FAILURE OF ISRAEL

This is fully confirmed and illustrated in the history of God's ancient people, the children of Israel. This is the history of another wretched failure, and one particularly humiliating and disgraceful. God Himself admits this.

Jehovah started out to make something extra fine of this people, as in Exodus 19:5-6 and Deuteronomy 14:2:

> Now therefore, if you will obey My voice indeed, and keep My covenant, then you shall be a peculiar treasure to Me above all people: for all the earth is Mine: And you shall be to Me a kingdom of priests, and a holy nation. These are the words which you shall speak to the children of Israel.

> For you are a holy people to the Lord your God, and the Lord has chosen you to be a peculiar people to Himself, above all the nations that are on the earth.

Yet, instead of that the people became worse than the worst of the heathen (Ezekiel 16), and He declares that His holy name was profaned among the heathen on their account (Ezekiel 36:16, 23).

Paul says of this same people that God's name was blasphemed through them. The culmination of Israel's failure was in the rejection and crucifixion of Jesus, and then they were cast off as the natural branches of the good olive tree, and the grafting in of the branches of the wild olive was accomplished in the call of the Gentiles during this present dispensation.

THE PRESENT WORLD FAILURE

Yet even this "Gentile church" was also to be a failure; that is, the nominal Christian "church." This is declared in several places, notably in II Thessalonians 2 where the great apostasy is set forth. That apostasy had already commenced in Paul's day, and now in our day it has culminated.

Before we notice further this last, let us consider how constant and universal failure is indicated in worldly matters and in the lives of people. The history of nations is a history of failure. We need only mention the names of ancient nations and cities to prove this to anyone familiar with history. Egypt, Nineveh, Babylon, Persia, Greece and Rome all stand for failure, decay and ruin. So also with human organizations of every kind – political, religious, commercial, or *any* other.

So it was in the individual lives of the so-called great reformers, philanthropists, religious leaders, statesmen, etc. They have always failed to effect those changes that they attempted. Some good has been accomplished – local improvements have been brought about, temporary advantage has been gained – but in the run of years conditions have dropped back into the same old ruts, and not in a few instances the last state has been worse than the former.

Take, for instance, the so-called social evil. The most strenuous efforts to abolish this evil have been made in all civilized countries from time almost immemorial down to the present, and yet the evil is still rampant and uncontrollable. The evil is ingrained in man's nature and can never be eradicated except through the resurrection. This brings us again to present times and conditions.

In the foregoing brief summary I am not trying to prove the proposition with which I started out, *i.e.*, that man's way is downward, universally and inevitably leading to failure. I write for those who are familiar with this fact and accept it. The point is this: Such failure is normal and intentional on the part of the Creator, a part of the process of creation – a process which will end in absolute success. In this success God is the One chiefly interested and responsible. Its non-attainment would involve His discomfiture and defeat – an outcome that is unthinkable. Temporary and intermediate failure as a means to an end is explicable and admissible, but final and eternal failure is impossible, because the ultimate issue depends on Him and on no other.

Are we living in a time of universal failure? Yes, most surely. I have no controversy with those who think otherwise. I write not for those who have no eyes to see and no mind to perceive and understand. This failure may continue for quite a long time with variations, for there has always been failure in the past, and there will be more failure in the future.

The outlook is by no means pessimistic. On the contrary, the brightest and most pronounced optimism may be indulged, for following the night comes the morning, the dawn, leading on to the perfect day.

The world has been led into a great darkness so it may see a great light (Isaiah 9:2). In the meantime, blessed are the eyes that perceive the present darkness as well as the oncoming light. Mind you, all of this is of God, for all things, absolutely all things, work together for good. The ruin that man brings on himself is made the occasion and the means of his extrication from that ruin. As it is written,

> *Your own wickedness shall correct you, and your backslidings shall reprove you* ... (Jeremiah 2:19).

> *O Israel, you have destroyed yourself; but in Me is your help* (Hosea 13:9).

God's way to light is through darkness. God's way to perfection is through error, defeat and deterioration. God's way to life is through death.

COUNTERFEIT CHRISTIANITY

Now, if you have eyes to see this, it will affect all of your observation and thought. For instance, you will know that there is no such thing in the world today as "institutional" Christianity, that is to say, no such thing as a visible Christian "organization." There are Christians in the world, thank God, a vast multitude of them, mostly uninstructed and ignorant, babes in Christ, carnal and not spiritual, and yet *"in Christ,"* but this Body of true Christians has no outward visible organization. They belong to no one particular sect or branch of a nominal church, but are partly included in them all and partly outside of them all. There is no "body" of believers of which it can truthfully be said, "This is the body of Christ, or the church of the living God, the pillar and ground of the truth."

All ecclesiastical and religious organizations and institutions are based on worldly principles, maxims and practices, and thus bear the "mark of the beast" that is characteristic of *"this present evil world."*

When you read in these days about "Christianity" or hear it discussed, you may know in the great majority of cases that it is "psuedo-Christianity" that is referred to – false, apostate Christianity.

The Christianity that the world knows anything about is the counterfeit. For many centuries there has been no visible Christian church, and the world has lost the knowledge of it. It began to deteriorate in the first century of its existence, and the declension has continued until our day. The ecclesiastical organizations of the entire nominal Christian church constitute *"the mystery of iniquity."* I am writing of the ecclesiastical organizations of all branches of the nominal Christian church, including Protestant, Roman Catholic, the Greek church of Russia and all of the sects and denominations, for they all come under one head as apostate, blind and darkened in their church governments and religious systems, copying after the world and not after Christ.

There are many mysteries in the New Testament, sacred secrets revealed to some and withheld from others (Matthew 13:11). The chief of these mysteries are the two contrasting ones, *"the mystery of godliness"* and *"the mystery of iniquity."* The former is God's secret purpose in this dispensation of free grace to take out a people for His name, the Body of Christ, the promised seed in which the rest of mankind are to be blessed and regenerated in the ages to come. The latter mystery is the essential apostasy of the nominal Christian church. *"The mystery of godliness"* is good in the form of evil. *"The mystery of iniquity"* is evil in the form of good, and the mystery of it is that all but the very elect are to be deceived in both, calling darkness light and light darkness.

Now notice how this present day failure and deterioration is manifested in the world in general. I speak very briefly and only in outlines, and again I say that I am not trying to prove the matter or to convince any who imagine that everything is going on prosperously and that all of the future is rosy and comfortable. Such ones are hopelessly deceived and cannot receive instruction.

International affairs, domestic affairs, religious matters, commercial, social, personal – or any other relationship – everything seems to be hopelessly mixed and in a most bewildering tangle, defying all efforts of extrication like an intricate knot that grows worse and worse the more one tries to untie it.

All we can do is to watch, fearing nothing, but rather with uplifted head and with joyful heart wait for the *"Desire of all nations"* (Haggai 2:7) to appear. In the meantime, we need not be surprised at *anything* that might take place, neither need we fear, for our Father is in full control.

> *The Lord on high is mightier than the noise of many waters, yes, than the mighty waves of the sea (*Psalm 93:4).

> *He who dwells in the secret place of the most High shall abide under the shadow of the Almighty* (Psalm 91:1).

It must be remembered that the history of mankind is one of continuous and unvarying failure, but it must also be remembered that the human race is only in the first stage of its development. The regular cycle of man's life includes two stages: first the natural, afterwards the spiritual – two planes.

> *Howbeit that was not first which is spiritual, but that*
> *which is natural; and afterward that which is spiritual*
> (I Corinthians 15:46).

The metamorphosis from the lower to the higher has not
yet taken place. God never intended that the physical
man should succeed. He must wait until after the change
comes. Then he shall have good success.

> *And when all things shall be subdued to Him, then*
> *shall the Son also Himself be subject to Him Who*
> *put all things under Him,* ***that God may be All in***
> ***all*** (I Corinthians 15:28).

Chapter 5

All Things Are of God

And all things are of God ...

~ II Corinthians 5:18

T here is no statement in the Bible, that was made by an apostle, that is more remarkable and even startling than this statement. When you think of it seriously, it seems as though Paul was very unguarded and careless in his language. We are apt to think that he ought to have modified and limited it in some way, for instance, all *good* things are of God.

But no, Paul makes the sweeping, unqualified statement, *"All things are of [i.e., out of] God."* Furthermore, so important did Paul consider this truth that he repeats it over and over again. The direct statement is made no less than six times in the writings of the apostle:

> *For of Him, and through Him, and to Him, are all things: to Whom be glory for ever. Amen* (Romans 11:36).

But to us there is but one God, the Father, of Whom are all things, and we in Him; and one Lord Jesus Christ, by Whom are all things, and we by Him (I Corinthians 8:6).

For as the woman is of the man, even so is the man also by the woman; but all things of God (I Corinthians 11:12).

And all things are of God, Who has reconciled us to Himself by Jesus Christ, and has given to us the ministry of reconciliation (II Corinthians 5:18).

In Whom also we have obtained an inheritance, being predestinated according to the purpose of Him Who works all things after the counsel of His Own will (Ephesians 1:11).

For it became Him, for Whom are all things, and by Whom are all things, in bringing many sons to glory, to make the Captain of their salvation perfect through sufferings (Hebrews 2:10).

Now, was the apostle careless and a little too bold in these utterances, or did he mean just what he said, and are they true, taken full strength? I say, without any hesitation, yes, to the two latter questions. The more we learn (the more revelation) of God's works and ways the more we shall understand that in a sense absolutely *"all things are of God."*

Chapter 6

We Are God's Workmanship

For we are His workmanship ...

~ Ephesians 2:10

A great and important truth is contained in this declaration, and one which practically most Christians deny. Theoretically all Christians believe that, in a *sense*, *"we are God's workmanship."* Yet in practice most of them deny it, and act as though they must *make* themselves and (in some cases) everybody else.

In other words, most Christians live as though the responsibility of their own development and perfection rested entirely upon themselves; and in addition to this they oftentimes act as though the responsibility of the world's salvation also rested upon them.

Understand that I am not speaking of the expressed *belief* of Christians, but of their *practice*. Now, the declaration – *"we are His workmanship"* – is most absolute and literal,

and we do not have anything to do with our own manu-
facture, so to speak, excepting to *"yield ourselves to God"*
(Romans 6:13).

> *God is not a man, that He should lie; neither the*
> *son of man, that He should repent: has He said, and*
> *shall He not do it? or has He spoken, and shall He*
> *not make it good?* (Numbers 23:19).

God's Own veracity is at stake here; His Own reputation
and credit, so to speak, is involved. For His *Own* sake, He
will complete and perfect His work. The beginning, continuance and completion of the process of creation are
entirely of God. God is man's *proprietor*, and will surely
make the best of His property.

We *are* God's workmanship. We *are* God's husbandry,
God's building, clay in the hands of the Potter, that is, so
far as the final accomplishment of the purpose of God is
concerned. *"I am the First, and I am the Last,"* the Lord
says, and all of this is the creative process. If Christians
could only see this, they would never think of such a thing
as making man's perfection depend on himself, for surely
in His creative work God needs no assistance.

I take it that God has a definite purpose in the creation
of everything – a definite end in view – and that end is
certain to be reached sooner or later. In other words, every creature ultimately fulfills the purpose of the Creator
in its creation. For us to suppose otherwise would be to
suppose a failure on the part of the Creator, which is unthinkable. The believer's attitude toward God then might
be thus expressed:

"God has created me for a definite purpose. That purpose I shall ultimately fulfill in His economy. It is a wise and good purpose, one with which I should be perfectly satisfied and contented if I only understood it all. Toward that end I am continually moving. All things tend to advance me in that one direction, and I shall surely arrive. I shall surely fulfill the purpose of my creation, and all I have to do is to leave myself in His hands as clay in the hands of the potter to be fashioned according to His will."

It is a great satisfaction and pleasure to think of our relationship to God in this light. For God has something in His mind to make of me, and I shall surely become that something. Furthermore, since God is wise and good, that something will please and satisfy me perfectly. When I reach the place for which God created me, and for which He fitted me, then I shall have no regrets that it is not another place. I shall realize that it is my place and shall be *satisfied,* perfectly satisfied with the accomplishment of the ever blessed and good will of God *in me.*

I am a seed, destined to a certain result ultimately. The seed may pass through many adversities in reaching that result, like the seed in the hand of an Egyptian mummy lying dormant for a thousand years, but still its end is fixed, and that end it will reach, and none other. I may frustrate the *grace* of God (as in Galatians 2:21), but I cannot frustrate His *will.*

I may be disappointed many times in failing to be what I would *like* to be, and what I *imagine* I might have been, and so my experience will correspond to the poet's words,

Of all sad words by tongue or pen,
The saddest are these – it might have been.

This experience is a part of my training, and by it I am continually being advanced toward what *I am to be* in the providence of God.

Let no one say, "This is fatalism." Nay, it is "Godism" – if I may reverently use such an expression. None need fear a fatalism that makes God supreme, absolute, almighty. In the foregoing remarks I am dealing with finalities. He is *"the First and the Last"* and He has His way ultimately. He is *able* to subdue – that is, to harmonize – *"all things to Himself"* (Philippians 3:21; Colossians 1:20). He Himself is love, and love has only one way of subduing – by harmonizing. This glorious consummation will be reached when *"all* are gathered together in *one"* (Ephesians 1:10) and God is *"All* in *all"* (I Corinthians 15:28).

Thus may the trusting child *rest in God* both for himself and for the *whole creation*, and with the utmost confidence he may commit all of his interests to Him *"as to a faithful Creator"* (I Peter 4:19).

Chapter 7

Trusting

1 desire to bring the subject of *Faith* right down to our everyday life, so that each reader may be led to *Trust* the Lord more fully.

FAITH AND TRUST

There is a difference between faith and trust. We may have faith in a person, and yet not be willing to trust him very much. We might believe a person to be very honest and upright and yet not be willing to trust to his keeping of our property or worldly reputation.

Trusting a person implies committing to his care something of our own; and the strength and fullness of our trust will be indicated by the value of the thing committed. We would trust a child with a few pennies to buy some small thing at the store, but we would not trust him with a large sum of money to transact important business.

We might trust our neighbor with some small commission, say to buy us a few dollars' worth of goods in a neighboring city, but we would hesitate to trust him further. The merchant might trust his confidential clerk with important business matters involving the risk of immense sums of money, and yet not be willing to trust him in some other things.

Sometimes we have a friend whom so far as his honesty and good intention is concerned we would trust to any extent – property, business, honor and life itself if need be. Such a friend you cannot trust in all things; there will be some lack in judgment, perhaps, or knowledge, or experience, or self-control, or some other defect that, while you have the most perfect confidence in his fidelity and good intention, prevents you from trusting him in all things.

What a wonderful thing it would be if one had a friend that he could *fully* trust in *all* things! One whom he knew would not fail him in *any* circumstance, either in good will or in ability. Ah, what a prize such a friend would be! How safe would be the possessor of such a friend! How comfortable, happy and secure! He would know that whenever trouble or difficulty came, all he would need to do would be to refer it to his friend, leave it in his hands, and then stand by and see *him* manage it. Would not that be grand? Oh, that we all had such a friend as that!

THE TRUSTWORTHY ONE

Well, have we not such a friend? Tell me, can human tongue find language wherewith to clothe a being with all the qualities of a perfect friendship, and not find even that ideal friend overtopped, and infinitely surpassed by the great, loving Friend of all, the *Father* of the human race? "No," you say, "of course not." Yet there is a lack about this divine friendship that *every* human heart feels. It seems intangible, far-away, unavailable and inoperative.

We have a theoretical, intellectual belief in God, but *"in works we deny Him."* That is to say, many a nominal Christian too, is yet practically an atheist, for the simple reason that the existence of God, with all of His attributes of goodness and mercy, crowned with unchanging love, is to him only a religious dogma, and not a living, everyday reality.

They would know how to appreciate, and how to use a true friend of flesh and blood, but how to make any good out of the friendship of God is entirely beyond them, though intellectually they do not doubt that friendship. Their faith in Him is merely intellectual, there is but little, if any, heart-trusting.

TRUSTING GOD

Now why is this? Why do we not *trust* God? For the very same reason, I answer, that we do not trust strangers, *because we are not acquainted with Him.* The great prerequisite to a perfect trust is a perfect acquaintance – a thorough knowledge of the person to be trusted. Everyone will see this truth at once. Furthermore, we must become acquainted with Him for ourselves; no second-hand knowledge will do, however exact and truthful it may be; no mere introduction, or verbal description of His excellences will satisfy us. We must know Him for ourselves, and know Him long enough to make sure that we can trust Him.

This is most certainly true in our relationship to one another, and it is no less true of our trust in God. Intellectually the Christian believes that God is his best friend; so other Christians have told them; so the Bible plainly teaches; and so they profess to believe – yet they do not trust God. They have some little *faith* in Him, they believe in Him, after a fashion, but they do not *trust* Him, *i.e.,* they do not commit themselves and all of their interests to Him, and rest in the assurance that He will manage all things well. All of this for the simple reason that they are not acquainted with Him.

They have some slight knowledge of Him; they know something about Him; but they do not know *Him.* They are not personally acquainted with the Father. Oh, it is no use, you cannot trust anyone you do not know. If you know not God, then you do not trust Him; and you cannot trust Him, for as yet He is a comparative stranger to you; and we do not trust strangers however much we may believe in them. *Get acquainted with God, and trusting Him will come as natural as breathing.*

GET ACQUAINTED WITH GOD

Now a practical question. How shall we get acquainted with God? How can we come to know Him, so as to fully trust Him?

I will try to answer this question. The only way we can know God is through the truth. *Christ* is *"the Truth"* (John

14:6). He is the living Word, and *"the Word was made flesh and dwelt among us."* We can get near Him, for He is bone of our bone and flesh of our flesh, and through Him – *"the Way, the Truth, and the Life"* – we shall at last get to know God, for *"no man knows the Father save the Son, and he to whom the Son shall reveal Him."*

Since we have Christ no longer among us in the flesh, it seems as hard to get to a risen and ascended Jesus as to God Himself. What shall we do then? Turn to that best embodiment of the truth that still remains with us: the Bible. As the Word incarnate is absent from us, we then turn to the written Word for the light that we need to lead us to God.

We know that the one great central idea of all Scripture is *Christ.* He is the fulfillment of all of the law; the anti-type of all types; the substance of all shadows; the theme of all prophecies; the subject of all Bible history; the center of Christian life and experience.

Studying the Scriptures then will be studying Christ; and learning of Christ is learning of God, since the former is the *"express image"* of the latter. Here, then, is the solution of our question, how shall we get acquainted with God? – Through the truth as set forth in the written Word.

Not that God does not reveal Himself to us in other ways than through the Scripture, for *"the heavens declare the glory of the Lord, and the firmament shows forth His handiwork. Day to day utters speech, and night to night shows knowledge."* Happy is he who can see God in *all* things, as He most certainly is, since *"all things are of God."*

The heavenly bodies, the solid earth, rock, hill and dale, tree, flower and shrub, lofty mountain and rolling ocean, the tiny blade of grass, and the pebble on the shore, the city full and the country waste – as well as all events great and small – all of these, each and every one, speak of God, million-tongued, and he who has eyes and ears to see and hear the divine in the human, the Godlike in the commonplace, he shall realize how wonderful is the truth of God's omnipresence; and instead of asking with Job, *"Oh that I knew where I might find Him"* (Job 23:3), will rather say with David, *"Whither shall I go from Your spirit? Or to where shall I flee from Your presence?"* Yet such power of seeing God in everything comes not except by long living in the way of truth. It is through experience that we must *grow* up by gradual development. We can no more jump into it at once than can the child leap at once into man's estate.

THE TRUE GOD – FROM HIS WRITTEN WORD

The written Word comes first, then, as a means whereby to know God; it is a revelation of God's will to man. It interprets His thoughts, His purposes and methods, and thereby makes God known to us, though we must needs have a true interpretation of that word.

The great mass of Christians do not know God so as to trust Him, not only because they have not the *truth* in regard to Him, but also because they believe many *lies* about Him. They are led astray by their "blind leaders." It is a wonder that Christians trust Him as much as they do, when by their horrid ideas of Him they make Him out to be anything but a God of love, worthy of trust.

The great majority profess to believe that by a perpetual miracle He will eternally keep alive myriads in hell for the sole purpose that they may suffer. Believing this and many other equally absurd and unscriptural things, it is a wonder that they have any love at all for the monster their theology makes God to be; and as for trusting such a being, the idea seems impossible.

With such a faith one might trust *Christ* and love *Him*, but the only feeling toward God possible under such a system of religion would seem to be one of dread and apprehension. Fortunately most Christians' hearts are better than their heads, and so with a happy inconsistency – not because of, but in spite of their theology – they love and trust God a little, though far beyond what anyone would suppose possible, knowing what they profess to believe of Him.

Oh, but how would their love and trust be augmented, from a smouldering spark to a glowing blaze, could they but see and understand the real truth concerning *"Our Father in Heaven."*

My purpose has been from the first to set forth those truths of God's word essential to such a knowledge of Him as will make us willing to trust Him fully. How wonderfully, for instance, does the great truth that *"all things are of God"* help us to trust Him!

If some things were *not* of God, that is to say, if some things took place independent of His will, or without His notice, or contrary to His purpose, then, though we might have perfect confidence in His good intention, we could not trust Him fully because we should not know what might happen to thwart or disarrange His plans. Yet when we know that *"He works all things after the counsel of His Own will"* – when we *know* this and realize it as a living *truth* – then we are ready to trust Him with all of our interests because we see that He is worthy of our trust; that as He cannot fail from lack of kindness and love, or from lack of wisdom and knowledge, so He cannot fail from lack of power and authority. It is He Who *controls* all things, *orders* all things, and when such power is directed by infinite wisdom and boundless love, we have a Being Who is worthy of the fullest trust, and Who is sure to receive it from all who know Him.

MOST ARE DEPENDED UPON CIRCUMSTANCES

And we know that all things work together for good to them who love God, to them who are the called according to His purpose (Romans 8:28).

With most people their happiness and comfort depends on their circumstances. Hence, since circumstances are very changeful, and for the most part entirely beyond our control, our happiness is very precarious; and the happiness of such ones, even when surrounded by the most favorable circumstances, will be more or less marred by the ever-haunting fear of possible impending calamity.

If there was any way whereby we might rise superior to circumstances, so as to be perfectly independent of them, then we should not have such fear, and our happiness would be unalloyed. Still, there is only one Being Who is thus superior to circumstances: the Maker of circumstances, the Director and Controller of *all things*.

What shall we do then, puny little boats as we are, tossed on the wide sea of life by ever contending influences, driven hither and thither by ever shifting circumstances, knowing not what a day may bring forth, nor how soon the red wine of our enjoyment may be turned into the bitterest gall of blasted hopes and thwarted purposes? What *can* we do but coldly wrap around us the mantle of a dull indifference and, reckless of the future, enjoy the present as we may?

Ah, but there is something better that we may do. We may take our place under the shadow of God's wing – yes, creep into the bosom of His love, and be as independent of circumstances as He is. How? By simply considering that *every* circumstance is the expression of His will, *i.e.,* the expression of His wisdom and love, and so most certainly a *blessing*, whether in disguise or otherwise.

I want the reader to notice this point particularly as it is the only secret of a restful, happy life. We can never be happy until we triumph over circumstances. We cannot control circumstances, but if we have a perfect trust in Him Who *does* control them, *we* can triumph over them through that trust, as completely as *He* triumphs over them by this power.

Such a trust, and consequently such a triumph, depends upon knowledge of God, acquaintance with Him, and can come only as the outgrowth of such knowledge. I will try then to help the reader to the knowledge, that he may ultimately possess the trust and the consequent peace and joy.

Probably *every* one has had the following experience: Events have occurred in their lives that have seemed at first very great calamities, but have afterwards proved the greatest of blessings. We have complained and wept and been bitterly disappointed, and perhaps rebellious over something that perhaps has afterwards proved to be one of the greatest blessings that we ever had, so that we look back on it in after years with joy and thanksgiving that we ever had such an experience. Thus in our own lives we have been convinced that troubles, sorrows and seeming calamities *sometimes,* at least, blossom into heaven's richest blessings, ultimately laden with *"the peaceable fruits of righteousness."*

Now, suppose we could be absolutely assured that this was the case *always?* – that no matter what occurred, however dark or calamitous it might appear, however grievous and distressing it might be, in the end it would prove a blessing, something that we should greatly rejoice over and be exceedingly glad that it had happened. If we could only be perfectly assured of this so that we had no doubt of it, then we should be independent of circumstances; for we should *know* that *nothing* could take place to our ultimate detriment.

Let it be remembered that all of us have had the experience, as the above, where seeming terrible misfortunes have been turned into ultimate blessings – where what at first has caused us sorrow has ultimately given us joy. Now we only have to extend this experience to all events – have *all* things work together for our good – in order to be in a position where we should feel perfectly independent of circumstances. Come what might we would be *sure* of being benefited in the end, and hence of course we should fear *no* event.

I need not tell any reader of the Bible that in the foregoing I have simply been describing the possible experience of all *"them who love God, to them who are the called according to His purpose."* All things, absolutely *all things*, work together for their good.

All things are for your sakes, *that the abundant grace might through the thanksgiving of many redound to the glory of God* (II Corinthians 4:15).

And not only so, but we glory in tribulations also: knowing that tribulation works patience (Romans 5:3).

For our light affliction, which is but for a moment, works for us a far more exceeding and eternal weight of glory (II Corinthians 4:17).

For I reckon that the sufferings of this present time are not worthy to be compared with the glory which shall be revealed in us (Romans 8:18).

Wherein you greatly rejoice, though now for a season, if need be, you are in heaviness through manifold temptations: That the trial of your faith, being much more precious than of gold that perishes, though it be tried with fire, might be found to praise and honor and glory at the appearing of Jesus Christ (I Peter 1:6-7).

But the God of all grace, Who has called us to His eternal glory by Christ Jesus, after that you have suffered a while, make you perfect, establish, strengthen, settle you (I Peter 5:10).

This is wonderful! It makes the one who fully receives it master of the situation. It is a triumph of faith, claiming complete dominion of God's universe, counting it ours on the strength of God's Word, and rejoicing in it as though we actually had it in possession, just as by faith we reckon ourselves "alive to God," "risen with Christ," and already "seated in heavenly places."

Such a life is a life of *trust*. One leading such a life can say with Paul,

> *I know Whom I have believed, and am persuaded that He is able to keep that which I have committed to Him against that day* (II Timothy 1:12).

Oh, the holy presumption and divine recklessness of such a trust! How sturdily and fearlessly it strides forward to meet the future! If things pleasant come, they are accepted, not with the surprise of unbelief, but as a matter of course. If things for the present grievous befall, they are received with a smile of anticipated triumph, even though the cheeks be wet with tears, and the heart wrung with agony from the stinging pain, for trust shall be the gainer in the end; *no other issue is possible.*

Though all of the forces of evil in the universe were let loose upon one trusting soul, they could but shower ultimate blessings on him, and hurry him on to his coronation. Oh, it is grand thus to be able, through the omnipotence of faith, to defy all enemies, sure, not only that they cannot ultimately harm you, but that they can do nothing but bless you!

THE WILL OF GOD

Now let us take another step in our effort to draw near to God, and to know Him, Whom to know is life eternal: *The Christian's Home is the Will of God.*

I would have every reader realize something of the unspeakable preciousness of God's will. Most Christians are afraid of His will. It seems to them something fearsome, so strict, and severe, and uncompromising. This, again, is because they do not know Him. When we come to know Him and trust Him, His testimony will be sweet to us because we shall then realize that it is the expression of His love (His being), and just the thing we should ourselves choose, could we but see the end of all events as well as He does.

As another has said, God's will is not a burden to carry but a pillow on which to rest. Mark this also: whatever comes to us is according to His will, and hence for our good. Nothing can happen contrary to His will. Is God's will done on earth? Yes, most assuredly.

Why then the prayer, *"Your kingdom come, Your will be done on earth as it is in heaven"*? If His will *is* done on earth, why the *prayer* that it may be done? God's will is *not* done on earth *as it is in Heaven*; and yet we *know* that God's will is done on earth in some sense, for we are told so in just so many words. *"He works **all things** after the counsel of **His Own will.**"*

If God's will is not done on earth, then whose is? The devil's will? The will of wicked men? If you say yes, then I ask, is God's will then thwarted or resisted in whole or in part? Are there any creatures that can override the will of the Creator? No, verily; such a condition of affairs would throw us back in "chaos and old night," and leave us uncertain aboutwho was ultimately to triumph, God or the Devil.

No middle ground can be taken, God is God. His will is never thwarted, therefore all things must be in accordance with His will, and hence tending to the fulfillment of His purposes of grace and love. It *must* be, as the Bible declares,

> *He does according to His will in the army of heaven,*
> *and among the inhabitants of the earth; and none*
> *can stay His hand, or say to Him, what are You do-*
> *ing* (Daniel 4:35).

God's will, then, is done even now. It cannot be otherwise, but it is not yet done *as it is in heaven*, voluntarily, and from the pure motive of love; but it shall be, so sure as Christ's prayer cannot go unanswered. Here again then we see what full ground we have for trusting God. All that comes to us is by His appointment, and for our good.

Of every trial and vexation, great or small, that we meet with from day-to-day we may say, "This is the will of God; the Father presses this cup to my lips; He puts this thorn in my way; He appoints this storm, this trouble, this sorrow; and so doing He says, 'take this bitter medicine, My child, it is not pleasant but it is needful, and therefore because I love you I cannot withhold it.'"

How foolish we are to resist! Like the sick child who struggles against the loving ministrations of its mother; rather should our attitude be as expressed by David, *"I was dumb, I opened not my mouth, because You did it"* (Psalm 39:9).

TRUST SPRINGING UP SPONTANEOUSLY

Thus a knowledge of these glorious truths brings God near to us, makes Him known, and trust springs up spontaneously. If we thus understand something of God's ways and purposes, and thereby get acquainted with Him, we shall surely trust Him, not only in the seemingly great matters of life but in all of the little everyday affairs.

Here is where many fail; they do not see that God is in all things; in their common household affairs – cooking, cleaning, or minding the baby: in business matters – on the farm, in the counting room, the work shop, or the study.

Do you know how to take a care to the Lord and *leave it with Him?* Many take their cares to the Lord, but keep on bearing them just the same, and the Lord lets us stagger along under these needless burdens because so shall we the sooner learn to cast them on Him.

> *Cast your burden on the LORD, and He shall sustain you: He shall never suffer the righteous to be moved* (Psalm 55:22).

How wonderful is the promise! *"Cast your burden on the Lord and"* – He will bear it for you; that is what we should *expect* it to say, and that would be blessed; but it says more than that. *"Cast your burden on the Lord, and He shall sustain **you**."* He will carry your burden *and you too.* Yet many of His children are so distrustful that they will not even let Him carry their burden. This is a real practical truth. Our burden is that which frets and irritates us; not the *hard* work, but the *constant* worry *that* is our care, and that is what we are to cast on the Lord and *leave* with Him, at the same time letting Him take charge of ourselves.

Casting all your care on Him; for He cares for you (I Peter 5:7).

Be careful for nothing; but in every thing by prayer and supplication with thanksgiving let your requests be made known to God (Philippians 4:6).

RESTING IN HIS WILL

Let me say further that there is not the slightest occasion for any anxiety or laborious exertion to know God's will. A brother wrote to me a few days ago that he was "earnestly waiting on God to know His will." From the gist of the letter it was plain that the brother was anxious to do a certain thing, but the Lord did not seem to open the way so that he could do it, and he was earnestly waiting on God, not so much to learn His will, as in hopes that He *would* open the way.

There is not the slightest need of such exercise. Be free with your Father; if He gives you no special clue of His will, do what you can, or what seems best according to your own judgment, or do nothing. Doing nothing is usually the hardest thing to do, and yet sometimes it is the only thing we can do.

*… Having done all, to **stand**. **Stand therefore** …* (Ephesians 6:13-14).

*But they who **wait** on the LORD shall renew their strength; they shall mount up with wings as eagles;*

they shall run, and not be weary; and they shall walk, and not faint (Isaiah 40:31).

Be still, *and know that I am God: I will be exalted among the heathen, I will be exalted in the earth* (Psalm 46:10).

*Or ministry, let us **wait** on our ministering ...* (Romans 12:7).

If that is God's will – to do nothing, to stand and wait – then in so doing you are just as perfectly following out the will of God, as though you were engaged in the most active service. Some Christians act as though they believed that if they did not keep constantly *doing* – "working for the Lord," they call it – that the Lord's cause would immediately begin to lose ground. With the most strenuous and persevering efforts they just barely manage to keep "the car of salvation" moving on. Should they relax their exertions, that vehicle would not only stop but immediately begin to slide back. These ignorantly zealous (Romans 10:2) persons think altogether too much of themselves. According to their idea it would seem to be a marvel how ever the Lord got along before they were born, and almost a dead certainty that He will have to suspend operations altogether after they are dead.

To all such ones the Lord says, *"Be still, and know that I am GOD."* They do not keep still long enough to find that out in the sense intended here, for the verse goes on to say, *"I will be exalted among the heathen, I will be exalted in the earth."* What? The Lord be exalted in the earth if they keep *still!* That cannot be, they think. Let me assure you, my dear perspiring brother or sister, that the Lord's cause will not suffer in the least, and you will be a great gainer if you will give over your air-beating (I Corinthians 9:26) for a little while, and take time to cultivate the Lord's acquaintance.

Study and *"Search the Scriptures,"* for they testify of Him (John 5:39) – knowing that all revelation comes from the Revelator, Christ Jesus. Trust that He will reveal something of His methods and plans, and then you will begin to see how foolish is the greater part of your sweating and straining, and how thoroughly *"all things are of God."*

Instead of talking and thinking so much about your *own* work, you will be able to say with the Psalmist,

> *You, Lord, have made me glad through Your work: I will triumph* [not in my own work but] *in the works of Your hands. O Lord, how great are Your works! and Your thoughts are very deep. A brutish man knows not, neither does a fool understand this* (Psalm 92:4-6).

It is the knowledge of *this* truth, that God is *"working salvation in the midst of the earth"* (Psalm 74:12), that gives calmness, tranquility and confidence, while others are in a perfect fever of excitement. Those who *know* God will *trust* Him, and such will enjoy *"the peace of God."* While others fret, fume, tug and strain, working hard but to no purpose because through their ignorance they are out of God's order, they shall be *resting* in the Lord and waiting patiently for *Him.*

> *Rest in the LORD, and wait patiently for Him ...* (Psalm 37:7).

When He gives quietness, who then can make trouble? (Job 34:29).

I would have every Christian see that God is managing in this world, as well as *"in the army of heaven."* Without the least interruption or hindrance His plans are being carried out, always and by all things, so that there is not the slightest occasion for worry or anxiety on that score.

As for God, His way is perfect ... (Psalm 18:30).

So far as we ourselves personally are concerned, as we get acquainted with the Lord and come to know Him better and better we shall trust Him more and more fully, realizing that our experiences, whether for the present, joyous or grievous, must be in accordance with God's will and hence sweet, and good and precious.

Oh, the blessed will of God, who would fear it, knowing that it is always the expression of His love! Take refuge then, tried and weary soul, in this great truth: God's will is being done *even now* in you, toward you, and around you in the world. *"All are His servants"* (Psalm 119:91), whether voluntary or involuntary, and no creature shall move a finger except as the Creator wills, hence you can fully trust Him, without fear, knowing that your hardest trials are your greatest blessings, as you will fully realize in the end. Make His will your home then, and look to that glad hour when His will shall be done in you, and in all, *"even as it is in heaven."*

Chapter 8

The True Basis of Redemption

You wilt have a desire to the work of Your hands.

~ Job 14:15

Showing that Redemption is a part of Creation, and hence its successful issue depends not on the creature, but on the **Creator.** He will have a desire to the work of His Own hands.

If a man dies, shall he live again? All the days of my appointed time will I wait, until my change comes. TYou shall call, and I will answer You: You will have a desire to the work of Your hands (Job 14:15).

Here in this passage is expressed THE TRUE BASIS OF REDEMPTION – *"You will have a desire to the work of Your hands"* (Job 14:15).

It is only as we recognize man as the work of God that we can understand his redemption. When I say man, I mean not merely Adam, the first man, but all of the redeemed, as finished, in the image and likeness of God. To the whole redeemed race, thus finished, the words of the apostle are applicable – *"We are His workmanship, created in Christ Jesus to good works, which GOD has before ordained that we should walk in them"* (Ephesians 2:10). Hence, in order to understand *redemption* we must understand *creation,* for the former is simply one step in the process of the latter. Let's then look first at the subject of creation.

CREATION

The common idea is that God created man perfect and complete in the garden of Eden, and thus started him all right; but evil invaded that peaceful and blessed retreat, successfully assailed the man and the woman, and the dreadful consequences were sin, alienation, the loss of paradise and universal death. Thus was God's handiwork marred and His plans disarranged, and now He must commence all over again, as it were, first, to repair damages and then to carry out His original plan as best He can. This is the common idea among the great mass of Christians, and yet the simple statement of it as above is enough to make one suspect that the idea cannot be just exactly right.

Is it so that God is altogether such an one as ourselves? Whose plans may be upset? Whose will may be thwarted? Who may be compelled to change His plan because of some interfering agency or evil power entering in and for the time being getting the better of Him?

Is it so? Why, no, we say; and yet what shall we do with the Bible story of the "fall of man" as we term it? Shall we make God responsible for it? If His will was not thwarted in that terrible fall, must we say that it was in accordance with His will? Many cannot say that – it seems blasphemous – and yet either that is true, or else His will was thwarted and His plans disarranged and upset by an evil power mightier, or for the time being, more cunning than Himself.

What shall we do in this dilemma? How shall we untangle this seeming snarl? Let us see how the Bible helps us.

I will first state the case as I understand it from the Scriptures, in my own language, and then give the Bible proof. First I would have the reader settle it in his mind that God is supreme.

GOD IS SUPREME

God is supreme in all realms and over all forces, evil as well as good. Nor would I abate one hair's breadth of this supremacy – let the consequences be what they may, for infinitely more direful are the conclusions flowing from such abatement.

If God's will has ever been thwarted, we have no positive guarantee that it will not be thwarted again. If His plans have ever been circumvented, disarranged and upset, the like may again take place. If evil has been more powerful than good at one time, or if God has been outwitted by evil or in any way hampered, constrained or limited by it at any time or under any circumstances, the like may again occur, and the pearly gates of the New Jerusalem, any more than the gates of Eden, may not be able to keep out evil, discord and death.

I ask the reader to consider this point carefully. Many shrink from taking the position that God's will is never thwarted but that, as the Bible expresses it, *"He works all things after the counsel of His Own will"* (Ephesians 1:11), because they say that such a view makes God responsible for the introduction of sin into the world and leads to other startling conclusions that seem impossible and even blasphemous.

Yet these persons do not consider the consequences of the opposite view that God's will is thwarted, and that He does not work all things after the counsel of His Own will; if that is so, then the future is doubtful, and the final triumph of the good and the perpetuity of that triumph is uncertain. No, no, it will not do: we must make God absolutely supreme. As He Himself says, *"I am God and there is none else"* (Isaiah 46:9), otherwise for all we know, there may be *"gods many and lords many"* (I Corinthians 8:5).

Just think of it a moment, for this point is so important that I will dwell upon it a little longer here at the outset. How did evil enter the world in the first place, if God did not permit it? Did *"that old serpent, the devil"* (Revelation 12:9; 20:2), enter Eden in spite of God? No, certainly not, for such a view would make the devil stronger than God, and we could not be sure who would finally triumph.

Did he get into Eden on the sly, outwitting God and getting the better of him? No, that idea would not do, for if the evil one has thus deceived the Almighty and cheated Him, what guarantee have we that he will not again get the better of Him? We must then take the ground that God permitted evil to enter the world, knowing of course full well what the consequences would be, and therefore in some sense and to some degree He is responsible for those consequences. Can you escape this conclusion except by detracting from the power and wisdom of God? The writer is free to confess that he cannot, nor does he wish to, since the Lord does not hesitate to take on Himself the responsibility of evil, as He does all other things; for He says, *"I form light and create darkness, I make peace and create evil. I, the Lord, do all these things"* (Isaiah 45:7), and we are told over and over again that *"all things are of God"* (Romans 11:36; I Corinthians 8:6; II Corinthians 5:18; Ephesians 1:11, etc.).

We do not relieve the Creator of this responsibility by saying that He was obliged to allow evil to enter the world in order that man, as a "free moral agent," might properly be tried and proved. God need not have created man at all had He not chosen to do so; but having created him, giving him the nature that He did give him, whether a "free moral agent" or whatever it might be, and knowing all of the consequences beforehand, for *"known to the Lord are all His works from the beginning"* (Acts 15:18), immediately He becomes responsible for those consequences. *He is the first great Cause,* and an intelligent Cause is responsible for all of the *effects,* however remote and indirect those effects may be.

This is generally held to be true even in the case of short-sighted man. If a human being starts a chain of events that in the end proves calamitous or hurtful to someone, if the matter can be traced back to the original mover, he is held responsible for all of the effects, even though he could not have foreseen them and did not intend the injury. Then how much more shall he be held responsible for all of his work who foresees and fully knows all of the consequences from the beginning to the end?

Let this point be settled then, that God is supreme; *"He works all things"* – absolutely all things, without any exceptions – *"after the counsel of His Own will"* (Ephesians 1:11). I exhort the readers to an uncompromising jealousy of this supreme sovereignty of God; begrudge to the Devil, or to any power of evil, the least share in this universal sway; emulate the example of Job in this respect when he attributed all that came to him, the evil as well as the good, to the Lord, saying, *"Shall we receive good at the hands of the Lord and shall we not receive evil?"* (Job 2:10).

As a matter of fact the Devil was the active agent in Job's calamities; but, as a matter of fact, the Lord was back of it all, and Satan could only move so far and in such a way as the Lord permitted (see Job 1:10-12; 2:6, 10). Hence Job was perfectly right in attributing it all to the Lord, and the Devil did not even have the satisfaction of being recognized at all, but he drops out of the narrative altogether at its very beginning, and thus may he drop out of our lives and we may deal with God alone for He controls the evil as well as the good.

We need not fear to take this position. There is abundance of Scripture to warrant it, as will be noticed further on; but if we had no other Scripture than this case of Job, it would be sufficient warrant for us to take the position that evil is entirely under God's control and He uses it, as He does the good, for the carrying out of His Own gracious plans and purposes. The hard experiences of Job were a blessing to him in the end, and yet his calamities were the direct work of the Devil. So will it be, under God's direction, with all evil.

The Lord of hosts has sworn, saying, "Surely as I have thought, so shall it come to pass; and as I have purposed, so shall it stand; for the Lord of Hosts has purposed, and who shall disannul it? And His hand is stretched out, and who shall turn it back?" (Isaiah 24:24, 27).

The Most High lives forever; Whose dominion is an everlasting dominion; and His kingdom is from generation to generation; and all the inhabitants of the earth are reputed as nothing; and He does according to His will in the army of heaven and among the inhabitants of the earth and none can stay His hand or say to Him, "What are You doing?" (Daniel 4:34-35).

Woe to him who strives with his Maker! Let the potsherd strive with the potsherd of the earth. Shall the clay say to Him Who fashioned it, "What are You making?" Or Thy work, "He has no hands?" (Isaiah 45:9; read this whole chapter, and compare with it Isaiah 10:15 and Romans 9:9-24; see also Isaiah 43:13; John 19:11; Acts 4:27-28).

There are many other similar passages; let them all be looked up and studied so that this question of the absolute sovereignty of God may be settled in your mind once for all. Do not allow yourself to entertain so absurd a belief, as many do, that the jurisdiction of the universe is divided up between God and the Devil, the latter having exclusive control over a large portion from which domain the Almighty is entirely excluded, or in which His power is secondary or in some way restrained and limited.

The above Scriptures show that such a view must be false, and our reason confirms the same conclusion, for we have seen how disastrous would be the opposite position. Either God is supreme, or He is not the only God. If He is not "God alone" then there are many gods, and in fact there is no "One God." This point being settled we are prepared to take the next step.

THE NEXT STEP

Redemption is a part of the process of creation, and creation is God's work and not man's. I presume that no one will question the statement that creation is entirely God's work, but some may object to the statement that redemption is a part of the creative process, because the common idea is that redemption was a sort of an afterthought with God, brought in as a remedy for the evil that Satan had wrought. Just one Scripture will dissipate this idea, viz., that Jesus Christ is *"the Lamb slain from the foundation of the world"* (Revelation 13:8), and that God's people are chosen in Him *"before the foundation of the world"* (Ephesians 1:4; I Peter 1:20).

These Scriptures plainly show that the redemption by Christ was no afterthought, but fully contemplated in the original plan, *"before the foundation of the world."* We know furthermore that redemption is creation, for *"if any man be in Christ Jesus he is a new creature"* (II Corinthians 5:17), and this new creation is the originally contemplated completion of the old, according to God's order: first the natural, afterward that which is spiritual (I Corinthians 15:46).

Now the new creation is just as much God's work as the old. No one could recreate himself, any more than he could have created himself in the first place. The Bible is very explicit and positive on this point, and this is the main thought that I want to present to my readers. Here is the proposition: THE REDEMPTION OF MAN IS THE COMPLETION OF HIS CREATION, AND DEPENDS FOR ITS FINAL ACCOMPLISHMENT ON GOD AND NOT ON THE INDIVIDUAL.

This work will certainly be carried out to a successful completion because it is God's work. *"He will have a desire to the work of His own hands."*

THIS IS THE
TRUE BASIS OF REDEMPTION

According to the common idea, one's salvation is made to depend almost entirely on his own personal efforts. God has made all necessary provision: He has prepared the feast, spread the table, and sent out the invitation. Now if you will accept and persevere you will be saved; but if not, you will be lost and God can do no more for you.He has made all needful provision and now your personal salvation depends entirely on yourself. This is the way the matter is usually put, and thus God is practically left out of the question in the salvation of the individual. Each one is taught that his future well-being depends on himself personally. If he will fulfill certain conditions God will do His part; but if he fails in these conditions God can do nothing more for him, and all that he has done will go for naught so far as he personally is concerned.

The writer has often heard this idea presented to the people in just this style, and with the utmost emphasis and positiveness – your salvation depends on you, it is for you to say what your eternity shall be, etc.

We have already noticed how positively the Bible declares that God will have His Own way in spite of all opposing forces, and Paul declared that he was perfectly confident that *"He Who has begun a good work in you will perform it"* (Philippians 1:6). We should remember that the process and completion of the creative work is as much *of God* as its inception, and we should remember further that God's Own honor and credit are at stake in the successful carrying out of His plans; thus does He accept the situation, and hence declares that *for His Own sake* He will complete that which He has begun.

This is the thought contained in the Scripture quoted at the outset – *"You will have a desire to the work of Your hands."* It is as though a person should commence a work in which he took a great interest and should carry it on to a certain stage, and then lay it aside for some reason; he does nothing more to it for weeks, months or years perhaps, but still his heart is set upon that work, he is deeply interested in it, he longs to be at it again and to complete what he has begun; he has a desire to the work of his hands, his own character and reputation as a workman is at stake and he feels bound to complete the job. Some such thought as this seems to have been in the mind of the old patriarch when he uttered the words we are considering.

> *If a man dies, shall he live again? All the days of my appointed time will I wait, until my change comes. You shall call, and I will answer You: You will have a desire to the work of Your hands* (Job 14:14-15).

It is important to notice in this Scripture that Job bases his hope of a future life not on anything he had done, or might do, but on the fact of God's proprietorship of him. He seems to have reasoned thus: I am an unfinished piece of divine workmanship; the divine Workman would desire to finish His Own work; hence, though I die, I shall live again.

This was Job's hope; this is our hope; this is the hope of the world. When God said, *"In the beginning"* (Genesis 1:1), *"let us make man in Our image and in Our likeness"* (Genesis 1:26), He did not mean merely the first man, but He meant the race. That work began in Eden and has been going on uninterruptedly ever since; it has been completed thus far only in the case of one man, *"the Perfect Man"* (Ephesians 4:13), the Lord Jesus Christ, and hence He has become the pattern and the model after Whom all the redeemed shall be fashioned, so that when the question is asked, *"What is man?"* (Psalm 8:4; Hebrews 2:6), the answer is, *"the Man Christ Jesus"* (I Timothy 2:5; see Hebrews 2:5-10). Jesus is the only Man thus far finished, completed and perfected; He is the only One as yet in Whom the creative proposition has been consummated – *"Let us make man in Our image and in Our likeness"* (Genesis 1:26), for He is the brightness of the Father's glory and *"the express image of His person"* (Hebrews 1:3). The first man could not have been in the image and likeness of God in the same sense that Jesus was, because the nature of the two are broadly contrasted in I Corinthians 15:45-49:

> *The first man, Adam, was made a living soul, the last Adam was made a quickening* [life-giving] *spirit; howbeit that was not first which is spiritual, but that which is natural, and afterward that which is spiritual; the first man is of the earth, earthy; the second*

Man is the Lord from heaven. As is the earthy, such
are they also who are earthy; and as is the heavenly
such are they also that are heavenly; and as we have
borne the image of the earthy, so shall we bear the
image of the heavenly.

Thus we see that the first man could not have been in the full image and likeness of God, for he was made altogether unlike *"the second Man,"* Jesus, Who is *"the image of the invisible God"* (Colossians 1:15). Therefore when we read of Adam that he was made in God's image, we know that the statement must be taken prophetically and prospective- ly, for God *"quickens the dead and calls those things which are not as though they were"* (Romans 4:17). We know that He was made altogether different in nature from Adam, and we know that Christ is the pattern after Whom all of the redeemed are to be modeled; we also know that He is the *"the Perfect Man"* (Ephesians 4:13), *"The Man Christ Jesus"* our Mediator with the Father (I Timothy 2:5), the *"Man Whom God has ordained"* to judge the world (Acts 17: 31), and this same *"Son of Man"* will come again (see Revelation 1:13; 14:14; Matthew 10:23; 13:41; 24:27, 30, 44; 25:31, and many other similar Scriptures).

It is a noteworthy fact that the Scriptures emphasize the humanity of Christ far more than they do His divinity; He is divine – *"in Him dwells all the fulness of the Godhead bodily"* – but this truth is not made so prominent in the Bi- ble as the fact that Jesus was thoroughly human, bone of our bone and flesh of our flesh; His usual title in the New Testament is *"Son of Man"* and thus He usually styled Himself. Only four times does He call Himself the *"Son of God"* (Matthew 26:63-64; Luke 22:70), while He takes to Himself the name *"Son of Man"* some eighty times.

Thus does it most certainly appear that Jesus Christ is *"the Perfected Man,"* that He is a Man still – *"the Son of Man standing on the right hand of God"* (Acts 7:56), and that *"this same Jesus"* (Acts 1:11) will come again, the Man Whom God has appointed to judge the world. Hence the conclusion seems inevitable that Jesus Christ is THE FINISHED MAN, the One only Man Who has passed through the entire process of creation and reached the image and likeness of God.

Now, how did Jesus reach this highly exalted and glorious position as the first fruits and forerunner of all of the saved? Was it by His Own might and power? Did He create and perfect Himself? No, most emphatically no; it was *all of God*. Jesus was entirely *"God's workmanship"* (Ephesians 2:10) just like all of the rest of the redeemed. There is such a mass of Scripture to establish this truth that I will refer to it very briefly and leave the reader to study it out at his pleasure and leisure.

In the first place, God brought Him into the world (Hebrews 1:6; Luke 1:25); *"God was with Him"* (Acts 10:38). His entire career and everything that He did and said was *of God* and by His power. Jesus never claimed to perform His mighty works by His Own power. On the contrary, He expressly disclaims any such thing: He did His mighty works *"by the spirit of God"* (Matthew 12:28), the works that He did were not His Own works (John 9:4), the Words He spoke were not His Own words (John 3:34; 14:10; 17:8).

"It is My meat and drink," He said, *"to do My Father's will and to finish His work"* (John 4:34). Again He says, *"the Father Who dwells in Me, He does the works"* (John

14:10; see Acts 2:22); *"Jesus of Nazareth, a Man approved of God among you by miracles, and wonders, and signs, which God did by Him,"* etc. Christ was the agent, God did the mighty works *"by Him."* Again, to the same effect read Acts 10:38-42. Thus was Jesus *"the beginning of the creation of God"* (Revelation 3:14). God was His God and Father, just as He is our God and Father (John 20:17). His passion and crucifixion was *of God* (Acts 2:23; 4:27-28); so also His resurrection, and exaltation (Acts 2:24; Philippians 2:9), also His return to judge, reign and deliver *"the whole creation"* (Romans 8:19-20). Jesus was weak; He says, *"Of My Own self I can do nothing"* (John 5:19, 30; 8:28) none of us are any weaker than that. Paul says that Christ was *"crucified through weakness, but He lives by the power of God"* (II Corinthians 13:4); all of His power was of God, and even His life, for He says *"I live by the Father"* (John 6:57).

Now turn to Isaiah 42:1-12. Read the whole passage comparing it with Matthew 12:18-21, and see how thoroughly Christ's earthly career and final victory was *of God.* God *"made known to Him the ways of life"* (Acts 2:28) and *"upheld"* Him, and this was the reason why it could be said of Him, *"He shall not fail."*

> *I the Lord have called You in righteousness, and will hold Your hand, and will keep You* (Isaiah 42:6).

Thus Jesus had to pass through a process of growth and development, in order to reach the divine image and likeness, just as a man must, and every step of this process was *of God.* As a youth, *"He grew in wisdom and in favor with God and man, and the grace of God was on Him"* (Luke 2:40, 52). There were some things He did not know

(Mark 13:32), and He had to be instructed. Among the rest he *"learned obedience by the things that He suffered"* (Hebrews 5:8). He had to pass through a training process *"that He might be a faithful High Priest in things pertaining to God to make reconciliation for the sins of the people"* (Hebrews 2:17), and finally He was made *"perfect through suffering"* (Hebrews 2:10), *"and being made perfect, He became the Author of eternal salvation to all them who obey Him."*

All of this goes to show that Jesus, during His earthly life, was passing through a process of creation, and that this entire process in all of its length and breadth was *of God*. Jesus did not perfect Himself, but was *"made perfect,"* *"the Perfect Man,"* and thus perfected He became, as we have seen, the model and pattern of all of the redeemed; they must be perfected as He was and by the same power – the power of God – in order to reach the same goal, and their creation, like that of Christ's must be entirely of God, as it is written,

> *We are His* [God's] *workmanship, created in Christ Jesus to good works, which God has before ordained that we should walk in them* (Ephesians 2:10).

The point that I want the reader to see is that the perfection of man, the consummation of his creation in the image and likeness of God, is God's work, and as such is sure of being accomplished, because the Great Workman is interested in His work, He has a *"desire"* to it, and He will not begin what He cannot complete. For the creature to fail of the purpose of its creation implies a failure on the part of the Creator, and this cannot be in the government of God. *"My counsel shall stand,"* He says, *"and I* will do all My pleasure" (Isaiah 46:10); hence we may be sure that the ultimate purpose in the creation of everyone, whatever it may be, surely will be carried out; as the Creator cannot fail, neither can His creations. Thus does it appear that, in the final outcome of man's creation, the honor of the Most High is involved, and He is bound to make that outcome a successful and glorious one in order to vindicate that honor. There is abundance of Scripture to establish this point, and we shall notice it in the course of our discussion.

We have found that man is still in process of creation, and that the consummation of that creation depends on God, the Creator, and not on man, the creature. Now notice how this thought is brought out in the New Testament. We have seen that everything in the earthly life of Christ was God-wrought, so we shall see that everything in connection with Christ's work, the inception, process and consummation of the redemptive work is all *of God*; and, being so, a successful issue is absolutely certain. In the following Scripture let the reader notice especially how GOD is made the *prime mover* and *pre-eminent cause* of the whole redemptive work.

Jesus Christ is the *"Lamb of God"* Who *"takes away the sin of the world."* It was because God so loved the world that He gave His only begotten Son; etc. and therefore, *"God commends His love toward us in that, while we were yet sinners, Christ died for us"* and, *"In this was manifested the love of God toward us, because He sent His only begotten Son into the world that we might live through Him."* Again it is *"the Father Who has sent the Son to be the Savior of the world,"* and *"No man can come except the Father draws him."* Says Christ, *"All whom the Father gives Me shall come to Me, and him who comes I will in no wise cast out." "The gift of God is eternal life through Jesus Christ our Lord."*

Now see II Corinthians 5:17-21:

> *Therefore if any man is in Christ Jesus he is a new creation; old things have passed away, behold, all things are become new; and all things are of God, Who has reconciled us to Himself by Jesus Christ, and has given to us the ministry of reconciliation, to wit, that God was in Christ reconciling the world to Himself, not imputing their trespasses to them, and has committed to us the Word of reconciliation. Now then we are ambassadors for Christ, as though God did beseech you by us, we pray you in Christ's stead, be reconciled to God. For He [God] has made Him [Christ] to be sin for us, Who knew no sin, that we might be made the righteousness of God in Him.*

Truly, *"ALL THINGS ARE OF GOD,"* and *"We are His workmanship; created in Christ Jesus ..."* and again, *"You are God's husbandry, you are God's building."* Read also Romans 5, 8, 9 and 11, and many more Scriptures in the New Testament to the same effect.

I call the reader's attention to these passages in order that they may notice that the whole redemptive work is attributed *to God*. Christ is God's agent; God is the principal at every step, and it is His love and His power and His grace that is manifested throughout. He is *"God our Savior, Who will have all men to be saved and come to the knowledge of the truth"* (I Timothy 2:3-4).

How different is this scriptural view of the redemptive work from that false view that exalts Christ and vilifies the character of God, making the former (Christ) to be loving and gracious and the latter (God) harsh and implacable, a Being Who must be appeased in order to make Him willing to forgive the sinner. Thus is the Father and the Son presented in contrast, when in fact the latter (the Son) is an exact revelation of the former (the Father), and by the same false view the teaching of Scripture is reversed by declaring that Christ's mission was to reconcile God to man, when in fact the atonement is wrought out by God in Christ reconciling the world to Himself, and then beseeching individuals, through His ambassadors, to be reconciled to Him. Thank God for the truth.

There is one passage of Scripture that may occur to the reader that perhaps I ought to notice in this connection; it is Philippians 2:12: *"Work out your own salvation with fear and trembling."* To many this passage seems to make one's salvation depend entirely on his own efforts, that he is to work out his own salvation, *i.e.,* he is to save himself by his own works. Of course, it cannot mean this, for if it did it would contradict other Scripture which expressly declares that we are not saved by works but by faith – *without works.*

What, then, does it mean? Read the next verse. *"For it is God Who works in you both to will and to do of His good pleasure."* There you have it again. *"All things are of God."* When God works in us both to will and to do of His good pleasure, what part is there left for the individual to do? The willing and the doing is about the whole of it, is it not? Then if God working in you does both the willing and the doing according to His good pleasure, there is not much room for the good works of self. It is as the apostle says, *"I labored more than they all, yet not I, but the grace of God that was in me."* Thus even this text teaches the same doctrine that we have learned from so many others: our salvation is *of God.*

This is the consummation of creation, and the work of the Creator, just as much as it was *"in the beginning."* Then what shall we do with the other verse, *"Work out your own salvation with fear and trembling?"* Why, the meaning of this is plain enough – work out what the Lord works in; that is all there is to it. God is working in you both to will and to do of His good pleasure; now you work that out; let the life inwrought of God be manifested outwardly, that all may know that you have been with Jesus and learned of Him. You can only work out what God works in; you cannot work for your salvation, or secure salvation by working; but the salvation, *i.e.,* the life, that God imparts, we may manifest, and that is what the text enjoins that we should do.

Thus from the foregoing we arrive again at THE TRUE BASIS OF REDEMPTION: God will have a desire to the work of His hands. He takes an interest and a pride, as we say, in His Own work, and for His Own sake He will carry it on to a successful termination. Now we will notice how this is confirmed and illustrated in the Old Testament by God's dealings with Israel.

ISRAEL

As we read the history of this people it seems to reflect great dishonor on God, as a wasteful child brings disgrace on his parents. From the Old Testament account it appears that God chose this people out of all other peoples, and lavished on them great blessings and gave them un-usual privileges in His attempt to make of them some-thing extra, as one might say.

They were to be to Him a *"peculiar people,"* a *"kingdom of priests and a royal nation;"* they were God's son, His first born (Exodus 4:22); they were His vineyard toward which He had exercised the greatest care (Isaiah 5), and finally they are represented even as being married to God (Ezekiel 16). Yet, notwithstanding all of these blessings, this care and close relationship to God, this people turned out bad in every respect; they were always disobedient, perverse and rebellious, continually leaving the true God Who had done so much for them, and going after idols, and in every respect were a low, degraded, ungrateful, wicked people who finally rejected their Messiah and put Him to death. Thus they filled up the full measure of their iniquity, and were cut off and cast aside as rejected branches from a good olive tree (Romans 11).

All of this was greatly dishonoring to God. It was as though one should adopt a child and take the greatest care that it should grow up extra good, and it should turn out outrageously bad. The parents would feel disgraced and dishonored, and many would blame them for the waywardness of the child, believing that if it had had the right sort of training it would not have so widely departed therefrom. Now this is just exactly the view that is taken of the matter in the Bible. The Lord acknowledges that His name has been *"profaned among the nations"* and dis-honored by the perversity of His people, and when Moses pleads for mercy and forgiveness for them, he bases his plea on the same ground (see Exodus 32:12; Numbers 14:13-16; Deuteronomy 9:28; 32:27).

The reader will see from these passages that Moses pleads for the Lord's favor on the ground that His Own reputation was at stake, and that if He failed to accomplish what He had started out to do His name would be dishonored. The Lord apparently accepts this plea and grants the prayer of His servant. This is the point that I wish the reader especially to note: the final accomplishment of the purpose of God depends on Himself and not on man. The creature may fail, yet the Creator never fails; and no amount of blunders, mistakes, failures or perversions of the creature shall disarrange or thwart the plans of the Creator.

This is our hope; this is the hope of the world; this is THE TRUE BASIS OF REDEMPTION: Man is God's Own work. He has begun to create him in His Own image and likeness. He will surely finish the work, for He will have a desire to the work of His Own hands.

There is one very striking illustration of this in the early history of Israel. They came to the borders of the Promised Land and sent out the spies who (with the exception of Caleb and Joshua) brought back an evil report – *"we cannot go up and possess the land."* The people with their usual perversity accepted this report at once and said, *"let us go back to Egypt."* Thus, after all that the Lord had done for them, after all of His mighty power and special favor manifested in their behalf – sufficient it would seem to confirm their faith forever – still they were ready to throw all of this away, turn their backs on the Lord and go back to the land of darkness and bondage. It seemed like an utter failure of all of the Lord's efforts to make anything good of this faithless people. They were a base herd of ingrates entirely unworthy of the high destiny that Jehovah had marked out for them; let them go to their own destruction, the plan has failed so far as they are concerned.

It is just at this moment of dire disaster and cowardly failure – in the very midst of the apparent defeat of the Lord's most cherished hopes, and while He pronounces the doom of that disloyal generation – that He at the same time declares, in a sort of prophetic undertone, and yet with all the confidence of omnipotence, *"But,"* – notwithstanding this apparent failure – *"as truly as I live, all the earth shall be filled with the glory of the Lord."* Here again is the thought made prominent that the failure of the creature does not handicap the Creator; He has His Own way at last, and works His sovereign will just the same.

This episode in the history of God's ancient people, and the Lord's attitude toward them, is simply a type and sample of their whole career and of God's dealings with them: they always failed; their entire history is a series of blundering, stupid follies and rebellions; they were always breaking their promises; they were always going after other gods, and the Lord was continually chastising them until it seems as though He was tired of it, for He says by the mouth of the prophet, *"Why should you be stricken any more?"* as a father might say to a persistently wicked child.

The Lord knew that they were a stiff-necked, rebellious people from the beginning (Deuteronomy 31:16-29) and that they would keep it up to the end. *"Ye will revolt more and more;"* He says, and then He gives the reason: *"the whole head is sick, and the whole heart faint; from the sole of the foot even unto the head there is no soundness in it, but wounds and bruises and putrefying sores; they have not been closed, neither bound up, neither mollified with ointment."*

Thus it was through all of their history that they were *"joined to their idols."* They were *"transgressors from the womb,"* and finally their wickedness culminated in the rejection and crucifixion of their Messiah, whereon they were rejected and cast aside. Thus, apparently the Lord's experiment with this people utterly failed. He tried to make something extra out of them and they turned out even worse than the surrounding heathen (see Ezekiel 16:44ff). Was not this a disgrace and a dishonor on Him Who acknowledged Himself as their God and, in a special sense, their Father and even their Husband (Isaiah 54:5)?

Has the Lord's purpose concerning them failed? Has He thus been balked in His plans, and prevented from carrying them out because He could not make of them what He set out to make? No, not at all; the Lord knew before He began just how the experiment would turn out. It was no experiment with Him. *"Known to the Lord are all His works from the beginning."* He is not taken by surprise; He is not disappointed; He meets no unforeseen difficulties, nor unexpected obstacles, but everything is known and taken into account and provided for beforehand. Will the Lord yet vindicate His wisdom and power in regard to this people? Yes, He most certainly will. The Bible most positively teaches that the Lord will yet take this people in hand again, and then He will accomplish all of His will in them, and that He will do this on His Own account in order to manifest to all nations His wisdom and power. Now notice how all of this is brought out in the Scriptures. The Lord says, *"I, even I, am He Who blots out your transgressions for My Own sake and will not remember your sins"* (Isaiah 43:25).

Mark you, the Lord blots out their transgressions for His

Own sake. He is personally interested in the matter on His Own account, and therefore He blots out their sins. Now read the rest of the chapter and the first eight verses of the following chapter; read carefully, weigh every word and see how this great and comforting truth of God's interest in the work and the consequent absolute assurance of its final fulfillment is brought out.

Now see another remarkable passage to the same effect in Isaiah 48:8-11:

> Yes, you heard not; yes, you knew not; yes, from that time that your ear was not opened; for **I knew** [mark this] that you would deal very treacherously, and were called a trangressor from the womb. For My name's sake will I defer My anger, and for My praise will I refrain from you, that I cut you not off. Behold, I have refined you, but not with silver; I have chosen you in the furnace of affliction. For My Own sake, even for My Own sake, will I do it; for how should My name be polluted? And I will not give My glory to another.

In this passage again is set forth God's personal interest in the destiny of Israel, and the consequent assurance of His will being fully accomplished therein.

Now see another passage in Ezekiel 20. This chapter sets forth the same idea; the persistent wickedness of God's people. Nevertheless, God did not destroy them or cast them off nor visit on them all of their sin, for He had respect to His Own reputation which they had disgraced. Therefore, He wrought in their behalf for His Own name's sake that it should not be polluted before the nations among whom they were, and in whose sight He had made Himself known in bringing them out of Egypt. (See :9, 14, 22, 44).

The whole chapter brings out this truth, that God is personally interested in the outcome of His dealings with Israel, that He feels disgraced, as we might say, at their failure, and that for His Own sake He will yet work for them and bring them into harmony with Himself.

This truth is still more plainly and positively brought out in chapters 36 and 37 of this same prophecy of Ezekiel. The Lord tells how His people had defiled themselves and how He had chastised them, pouring out on them His fury and scattering them among the nations; and yet they profaned His holy name more and more wherever they went, and the heathen said sneeringly, *"These are the people of the Lord, and are gone forth out of His land"* (:20).

This was not so much a blaming of the people, as a sarcastic reflection on the Lord – these are the Lord's people; those whom He undertook to make superior to other people; see what they have come to, mark how well the Lord has made out with them, etc. Thus was the Lord's name profaned and disgraced, like as when they wagged their head at Jesus on the cross and said mockingly, *"He saved others, Himself He cannot save"* (Matthew 27:42; Mark 15:31; Luke 23:35).

Will the Lord let it go that way? Is He done with His people? Are all of His resources exhausted? Has He done His very utmost, and must He accept the inevitable and give it up as a bad job which He can never complete? Not so, by any means; whatsoever the Lord has set His hand to do He will surely carry through, *"and none can stay His hand or say to Him, 'What are you doing?'"* (Daniel 4:35). *"Has He said, and shall He not do it? Or, has He spoken and shall He not make it good?"* (Numbers 23:19).

So here in the prophecy we are considering, the Lord goes on to say:

> *But I had pity for My holy name which the house of Israel had profaned among the heathen, wherever they went; therefore say to the house of Israel, "thus says the Lord God, 'I do not this for your sakes, O house of Israel, but for My holy name's sake, which you have profaned among the heathen, wherever you went; and I will sanctify My great name which you have profaned in the midst of them, and the heathen shall know that I am the Lord,' says the Lord God, 'when I shall be sanctified in you before their eyes.'"*

God will be sanctified in Israel before all nations by carrying out His original purpose concerning them; and this He will do, not for their sakes, but for His Own sake; and He will gather them out of all countries from wherever He had scattered them and bring them into their own land.

> *Then will I sprinkle clean water on you and you shall be clean; from all your filthiness and from all your idols will I cleanse you; a new heart also will I give you and a new spirit will I put within you, and I will take away the stony heart out of your flesh, and I will give you a heart of flesh; and I will put My spirit within you, and cause you to walk in My statutes, and you shall keep My judgments and do them; and you shall dwell in the land that I gave to your fathers, and*

*you shall be My people, and I will be your God. I will
also save you from all your uncleannesses; I will call
for the corn, and will increase it, and lay no famine
on you; and I will multiply the fruit of the tree, and
the increase of the field, and you shall receive no
more reproach of famine among the heathen.*

Mark how the Lord says He will do all of this without any
conditions attached whatever – "I will cleanse you, I will
save you, I will cause you to walk in My statutes, and you
shall keep My judgments and do them." There are no "ifs"
about it; there are no contingencies; "I will do it, and you
shall do it," and the result:

*Then shall you remember your own evil ways, and
your doings that were not good, and shall loath
yourselves in your own sight for your iniquities and
for your abominations.*

Now why does the Lord do this?

*"Not for your sakes do I this," says the Lord God.
"Be it known to you; be ashamed and confounded
for your own ways, O house of Israel."*

Then He goes on to tell what He will do further, and adds:

*Then the heathen that are left around you shall
know that I the Lord build the ruined places, and
plant that that was desolate; I the Lord have spoken
it and I will do it.*

There is no doubt about it: it is sure to be done, for God's
Word never returns to Him void nor fails to accomplish

that whereto He sends it (Isaiah 55). He says, *"I have spoken it; I will also bring it to pass; I have purposed it, I will
also do it"* (Isaiah 46:11).

Language could not be plainer than the foregoing Scriptures
to express the thought of God's absolute sovereignty and
that He always has His Own way, that whatever His purpose is He carries it out and no failure on the part of man
can ever change the divine program, or in any way or in the
least degree thwart the divine will. God's Own honor and
credit is at stake: He recognizes it so, and speaks and acts
accordingly, and what seems like failure will yet be seen to
be a success so absolute and grand that only omnipotence
could compass it.

There was no failure in connection with this people from
God's standpoint. He knew from the first how everything
would turn out, and the lesson He would teach them, and
through them to the race – for all of these things which were
done for the admonition of later generations will be thoroughly learned (I Corinthians 10:11). Then in the future ages
He will yet make of this people a holy people, obedient and
faithful, and they shall walk in the way of His statutes and
keep His judgments and do them; they shall be ashamed
of their former perverseness and disobedience, and repent
them of all of their evil deeds, and God's name shall be sanctified in them, which once they profaned. Mark you, God
does all of this of His Own sovereign will and power; and not
for their sakes, but for His Own sake.

Here again is THE TRUE BASIS OF REDEMPTION: the will of God,
His Own purposes and plans, His Own almighty power,
unfailing wisdom and unalterable word, His proprietorship
of man – *"We are His workmanship."* He is personally in-

terested in the work and in its successful issue – His Own honor is at stake, He will do it for His Own sake – He will do it, and therefore it is absolutely certain of being done. Thus the final outcome depends not on man; you and I are free and responsible intermediately, and will be held strictly accountable for all of the deeds done in the body; but God is the first and the last; He has His way finally, and man has no power to stay His hand, or to say to Him, "What are You doing?" No act of the creature can alter or disarrange the final plans of the Creator.

DEATH

We must now go a step further in our study of this subject. It is the final one, and makes the grand truth complete. I want to show that *death,* any more than anything else, is no hindrance to the perfect accomplishment of the *ever* blessed will of God.

We have thus far said nothing on this point; and it may be that the reader, like the great mass of Christians, holds to the idea that death, physical death, fixes forever the destiny of everyone. One may change after death from bad to worse or from good to better – there may be progress in either direction, upward or downward – but there can be no change from bad to good, or from the downward road to the upward. This is the current belief, and it is supposed by many to be fully warranted by the Bible. As a matter of fact, this belief is a mistake; it has no scriptural support at all. What foundation it has is from human tradition.

In the few closing words of this work I will give some of the evidence to establish the truth that God in Christ is Lord of the dead as well as the living, and that though a man dies in his sins, still he is not beyond the reach of the ever merciful arm of the Almighty (Psalm 136).

We have found that God the Creator has His way, and carries out His purpose with reference to His creatures whatever may be their condition or circumstances. The plainest and most positive Scripture has been cited to prove the above. Now, if death fixes man's eternal destiny, the above would not be possible. Billions of human beings have died in the past in unavoidable ignorance of the true God and of Jesus Christ Whom He has sent, and millions are dying every day in the same condition.

If the doom of these countless myriads is sealed eternally, then two conclusions follow: either God's purpose in their creation was that they should come to just such an end as they have come to, or else His purpose has failed. His purpose cannot fail, for He says, *"My counsel shall stand and I will do all My pleasure"* (Isaiah 46:10). *"He works all things after the counsel of His Own will,"* i.e., in the final outcome God's will is accomplished. Neither can we accept the conclusion that these myriads who have lived in ignorance and sin, and died in darkness, and, according to the current belief, are therefore hopelessly lost, have hereby fulfilled the purpose of their creation. Such an idea is utterly contrary to the revealed nature of God and diametrically opposed to all of the teaching of Holy Scripture, wherein we are taught that God loves the world, that He sent His Son to be its Savior – *"the propitiation for the sins of the whole world"* – that the Son is the *"True Light which lights every man who comes into the world"* (John 1:9), and that, finally, the whole creation *"... shall be delivered from the bondage of corruption into the glorious liberty of the children of God"* (Romans 8:19-21).

Therefore, since we cannot accept either conclusion, we must also reject the premise; the only way out of this difficulty is to admit the possibility of enlightenment and salvation after death. Take for example the declaration that God will have *"all men to be saved and come to a knowledge of the truth"* (I Timothy 2:4). How can the will of God in this particular be carried out if death fixes the eternal condition of all, since the great mass of mankind have died, and are still dying, without any knowledge of the truth at all? This is so with many other Scriptures (John 1:9; Luke 2:10, etc).

Take the case of Israel that we have been considering. We know that God will carry out His will regarding them, notwithstanding all of their perversity and failure. Yet how can this be if He cannot reach the millions of this people who have died in the past? God did not have His Own way with them; and now their doom is sealed. Is it so? Not thus does Holy Scripture speak to the writer. We have seen what great blessings God has promised this people in the future. Do the ones to whom these promises were given, those who were living at the time, have no share in their fulfillment? Have they passed forever beyond the reach of all benefit from these gracious and wonderful words of future good, when they should be ashamed and repent of their wrongdoing? Do these words apply only to some future generation of this people who may happen to be living on the earth at the time of their fulfillment?

In answer to these questions read Ezekiel 37 – the vision of the valley of dry bones, and notice that *"the whole house of Israel"* is the subject under discussion, and that God promises to *"open their graves and bring them up out of their graves,"* and bestow on them the great blessings enumerated.

See also the remaining part of the chapter and notice how all Israel, both houses, Judah and Ephraim, are included, and God will bless them and save them and cleanse them, etc., and David shall rule over them, etc. Surely no one can read this chapter without being strongly impressed with the thought that there is a wonderful future for this people in which all of them are to share, even *"the whole house of Israel."*

Paul confirms all of this in Romans 11. I have not space to observe this wonderful chapter particularly, but recommend the reader to study it carefully verse-by-verse, for the light it gives on the gracious ways of God is marvelous; and notice especially that the apostle's conclusion is that *"all Israel shall be saved"* (:26).

I will throw out a thought here for the reader's consideration. I shall not be able to amplify it, but perhaps the reader will be interested enough in the subject to study it for himself. We have been considering the history of Israel in its past and the glorious prophecies of the future, solely with reference to this one people. I have no doubt but that these prophecies are to be fulfilled literally – they mean all that – but, mark you, they mean more. Israel stands for the race; the history of that people, their past and their future and God's dealings with them is but a sample and a type and a promise of the future of the race. Thus will God deal with mankind; through a similar experience shall they all pass unto a like glorious destiny. Without going into this subject further here, I will refer the reader to the following passages: Deuteronomy 32:8; Isaiah 19:23, 25; Romans 11 (the whole chapter); I Corinthians 10:1-11; etc. Thus understood, the history of this people becomes of universal interest, and thereby a reason appears why it should occupy four-fifths of the sacred writings. Yet we must now pass on to the final illustration of THE TRUE BASIS OF REDEMPTION.

SODOM

The force of the foregoing argument drawn from the history of Israel might be somewhat evaded by asserting that the promises of future good to this people are to be fulfilled only to the righteous portion of the race who may be living when the time comes for the complete fulfillment of these prophecies.

Now as if to nullify such a parrying of the teaching of God's Word, whereby the Holy One of Israel is *"limited"* (Psalm 78:41), the Lord has given us an illustration of this same truth which does not admit of any such explanation. In the case of the wicked Sodomites, there was no righteous among them at all; if there had been ten righteous persons in all of the cities of the plain of Jordan they would not have been destroyed (Genesis 18). Furthermore, if there are any future blessings for them, it must be for the wicked dead, for they were all destroyed – not one escaped; they all perished in their sins – and whatever of good or ill there is for them in the future must necessarily be posthumous (Luke 17:29).

The record of the exceeding wickedness of this people and their awful destruction is familiar to every Bible reader (Genesis 19). Yet it is strange how many there are, even those who are quite familiar with the written Word, who nevertheless have never noticed the wonderful prophecy of future restoration and blessing for these typical sinners. This prophecy is in Ezekiel 16.

I will briefly notice the leading points in the prophecy. If the reader will study all of the references and carefully consider the subject without prejudice, I think that he will admit that this prophecy, together with the connected passages referred to, fully warrants a hope of future good for "exceedingly" wicked Sodom (Genesis 13:13) and, by a fair inference, for all of the wicked dead.

Now turn to the 16th chapter of Ezekiel's prophecy and read it through carefully. You will notice that the first part of the chapter is highly figurative; but as we get along into the middle part it becomes less and less figurative, until in the latter part of the chapter the figure is dropped altogether and the statements are in plain and direct terms.

Sodom, Samaria and Jerusalem are three contrasted cities. Sodom and Samaria are the younger and the older, or (margin) the lesser and the greater sister of Jerusalem. The idea is that all three are of the same family in sin, but Sodom is the least guilty of the three and Jerusalem the most guilty, because the former city had the least light and Jerusalem the most; in fact the sin of Sodom was "a very little thing" in comparison to that of Jerusalem. We need not be surprised therefore, or in the least degree incredulous when we find future blessings promised to Jerusalem, if we find them also promised to less guilty Sodom.

We know that there are such blessings promised to Jerusalem; see, for example, the 40th and 60th chapters of Isaiah, the 30th and 31st of Jeremiah, the 20th and 36th of Ezekiel, the 2nd of Hosea, and many others; also the last part of this 16th of Ezekiel, as we shall notice presently. These are unmistakable promises of future blessings for

Jerusalem and Israel; but are there any such blessings for the wicked Sodomites? Read on in the chapter – :53 and the two following read as follows:

> *I will turn again their captivity, the captivity of Sodom and her daughters* [the cities of the plain], *and the captivity of Samaria and her daughters* [the other cities of Israel] *and the captivity of your captives in the midst of them; that you may bear your own shame, and may be ashamed of all that you have done, in that you are a comfort to them; and your sisters,* **Sodom and her daughters, shall return to their former estate;** *and You and your daughters shall return to your former estate.*

Now, what does this remarkable prophecy mean? What does *"turn again their captivity"* mean? This is explained in the next verse – *"return to their former estate."* What else can this mean, in the case of the Sodomites at least, but that God will bring these wicked people back again from the captivity of the grave (Ezekiel 16) and restore them to their former fleshly life? If not, then what?

Read the rest of the chapter and you will see that they are to be blessed and *"forgiven"* together with Samaria and Jerusalem. God will remember His covenant with Jerusalem *"in the days of her youth"* (:60), and will establish with her *"an everlasting covenant."* Then she shall remember her ways and be ashamed when she shall receive her sisters, the elder and the younger – Samaria and Sodom – and they shall be given to her for *"daughters"*; yet not by her covenant, that is, the old covenant which she had broken, but by a new covenant which He will establish with her. She shall know the Lord, *i.e.,* she shall have *"life eternal"* (John 17:3); and she will remember and be confounded and never open her mouth any more, when the Lord has forgiven her all of her sins.

There can be no doubt but that a future blessing is foretold here for Jerusalem, Samaria *and Sodom;* and in the case of the last named it must be a future blessing for the wicked dead; no other interpretation can be put on the passage unless it was forced on it. Why should we wish to put any other interpretation on it? Why should it be thought *"a thing incredible"* (Acts 26:8) that God should thus raise the wicked dead to be dealt with in grace and mercy? How else can the Word of God stand that we have been considering, that so plainly teaches, as we have seen, that God has His Own way at last and brings His creation to a successful issue, completing and perfecting His Own workmanship?

Let us look a little further at the case of Sodom and see how reasonable this prophecy of its future restoration and blessing is, and how eminently in harmony it is with other Scripture. In :49-50 of this chapter *"the sin of Sodom"* is set forth, and we see that that sin is exactly the same as could be truthfully laid to the charge of every large city in the world today. Yet there is one sin, worse than all of the rest, of which Sodom was not guilty, but the modern cities of Christendom are guilty of that same sin – it is this: the sin against light, the misuse of special privileges, the rejection of the truth, the denial of Christ.

Sodom never had such opportunities as these and therefore could not commit these sins; but modern cities do have these privileges and are therefore more guilty than ancient Sodom; this was just exactly what made the difference between Sodom and Jerusalem, so that the sin of the former (Sodom) was *"a very little thing"* compared to that of the latter (Jerusalem). Does it not seem strange that Sodom should be eternally lost without ever having any opportunity at all to obtain eternal life, especially so since Jesus expressly tells us that if Sodom had had this light it would not have perished as it did (Matthew 11:20-24)?

On the ground that the doom of Sodom is eternal, the above considerations are inexplicable; but on the ground of this prophecy of the restoration and blessing of Sodom at some future time, every difficulty disappears, and we can plainly see how true it is that death cannot separate us from the love of God any more than *"any other creature"* (Romans 8:38-39).

It must not be overlooked also that this restoration of the wicked nations at some future time is not confined to Sodom alone. Moab, Ammon and Elam are to be similarly restored *"in the latter days"* (Jeremiah 48:47; 49:6, 39). Read carefully also the prophecy of Obadiah with reference to Edom, and note especially the last verse. Finally David makes this restoration of the nations universal when he says,

> *All nations that You have made shall come and worship before You, O Lord, and shall glorify Your name; for You are great and do wondrous things; You are God alone* (Psalm 86:9-10; c.f. Revelation 15:1-4).

Here, then, is the most positive evidence that the failure of the creature, even to the extreme of physical death, is no hindrance to the Creator in fully carrying out His original plan. Indeed, why should it be?

Is it because death is such a decided check to ourselves, and we stand so helpless and blank at the grave's mouth, utterly unable to go any further either in our love or hate, that we think God is equally helpless, and that death is to Him also a rock-bound coast with power to say to the great ocean of His mercy and love, *"thus far shall you go but no farther"* (Job 38:11)? Or, is God simply able to imprison His enemies eternally without being able through all eternity to make them His friends? Or, again, shall the skill and power of the Almighty be baffled and nullified by some millions of bits of crude material, successfully resisting His workmanship, rendering all of His gracious efforts vain, and turning out after all wretched failure and ugly monstrosities, so that no choice is left to the Creator but to give over His efforts, and thrust these failures out of sight, or crush them out of existence forever?

In all of these questions I am looking at the matter from God's standpoint solely, leaving out all consideration of man's "freedom" and "responsibility"; and this we have a right to do because He claims to be *"able even to subdue all things unto Himself"* (Philippians 3:21). He says He will *"reconcile all things to Himself"* (Colossians 1:20); that *"every creature"* shall finally praise Him (Revelations 5:13), and He will be *"All in all"* (I Corinthians 15:58).

When the Lord God Almighty makes such declarations as these it is not for mortal man to raise obstacles and suggest objections, and wonder how the Lord can do this and that. It is enough that He is able, and He will; *the how* we can leave to His Own infinite resources.

A GLIMPSE INTO THE HOW

We are not however left entirely in the dark as to *the how,* as we have seen from the foregoing considerations. God can punish for wrongdoing with the utmost severity, as in the case of Sodom, and yet when it pleases Him He can restore those who have thus been destroyed under the rain of His righteous wrath, and can bring them to Himself, accomplishing fully in them the original purpose of His creation.

Thus, *"He turns man to destruction and says, 'Return, you children of men'"* (Psalm 90:3). He kills and makes alive; He wounds and His hands make whole; He has torn and He will heal us (Deuteronomy 32:39; I Samuel 2:6). Blessed be His Name forever, His power is unlimited! We are the clay, and He is the Potter (Isaiah 64:8), and thus the Great God and Father of all is *"a Faithful Creator."*

A FAITHFUL CREATOR

Did the reader ever think of the significance of this expression? The apostle says,

> *Wherefore let them who suffer according to the will of God commit the keeping of their souls to Him in well doing, as to a Faithful Creator* (I Peter 4:19).

According to the prevailing theological ideas it would be difficult to tell what God, as a Creator, has to do with the above described circumstances. If it had said God our heavenly Father, or God our Redeemer, or something of that kind, it would be perfectly explicable; but our Creator! Why, we are apt to think that creation is something accomplished and in the past, and then it was marred and afterwards patched up – partially – the damage not being wholly repaired. Can you not see, friend reader, that this idea is a mistake? God is *still* our CREATOR. The work is not yet finished; completion and perfection is not something that man once had and lost, but it is yet before him. The Almighty is the Great Workman, and we are *"His workmanship."* Everything that comes to us is part and parcel of the *creative process,* and *all* tends to the *grand consummation* of the divine Artificer's glorious work.

GOD MY CREATOR

There is infinite comfort in this great truth. God as my Creator – still creating me – is responsible for my *final* completion. Hence that completion is *absolutely* sure.

I have therefore a *claim* on Him, I have a *right* to look to Him for help and succor in *every* time of need, and this claim, and this right, is fully recognized and acknowledged in this expression – *"A Faithful Creator."*

Ah, it is most blessed to be able to say in the midst of trouble and overwhelming sorrow – *"I am Your … Your hands have made and fashioned me … You will have desire to the work of Your hands"* (Psalm 119:94, 73; Job 14:15).

Thus did Moses plead with God, as we have seen, daringly urging, not the people's deserving, but God's responsibility, as if to say, "You have commenced this work, You are responsible for its completion"; and the Lord accepts the plea and acts upon it. So, later in the history of this same people, the prophet, although he fully confesses and deeply deplores the sinful, undeserving character of the people, yet he urges the same plea, and receives a similar gracious response.

Read Isaiah 63 and 64. First, we have that dreadful account of the treading of the winepress by the red-appareled One from Edom, and Bozrah, traveling in the greatness of His strength. Yet this account is sandwiched in between the description of this same personage, speaking in righteousness and mighty to save, and (:7), the mention of the *"loving kindnesses"* and *"great goodness"* of the Lord; and then, as though to account for this kindness and goodness toward such an unworthy people, the prophet says (:8), *"For He says, 'Surely they are My people, children who will not lie:' so He was their Savior."* An indulgent Father speaks of His children apologetically in such a way as He desires them to be, and hopes they will be; and then He continues,

> *In all their affliction He was afflicted, and the angel of His presence saved them: in His love and in His pity He redeemed them; and He bare them, and carried them all the days of old.*

Thus, He dealt with them in great mercy and love, because they were *"His people,"* and now note, *"But they rebelled, and vexed His holy Spirit: therefore He was turned to be their enemy, and He fought against them."* Notice again, *"Then He remembered the days of old, Moses, and His people, saying, 'Where is He Who brought them up out of the sea with the shepherd of His flock? Where is He Who put His holy Spirit within him?"* Thus He goes on appealing to the Lord on the ground of His proprietorship of them, and the fact of former mercy and love. Again in the :16 we read,

Doubtless You are our Father, though Abraham be
ignorant of us, and Israel acknowledge us not; You,
O Lord, are our Father, our Redeemer; Your Name
is from everlasting (Isaiah 63:16).

The prophet insists that God is their Father and Redeemer, although they had acted unworthy of the children of Abraham and had disgraced the name of Israel;
yet still they would hold on to their relationship to God.
Then again in the last verse of this same chapter, *"We*
are Yours." Notice the significance of this continued re-
iteration of God's proprietorship of them, both as Father
and as Owner, together with unstinted self-condemnation
and humble confession of sin; and yet – *"We are Yours"*;
"Doubtless You are our Father" – there is no doubt about
it, notwithstanding its apparent unlikeliness: we are *"the*
tribes of Your inheritance," "the people of Your holiness."

The same thought runs through the next chapter (64), and
the same assertion of relationship to God culminates in
:8-9.

Now, O Lord, You are our Father, we are the clay,
and You our Potter; and we all are the work of Your
hand. Be not wroth very sore, O Lord, neither re-
member iniquity forever. Behold, see, we beseech
You, we are all Your people.

How daring, and seemingly presumptuous is the claim!
How vivid the expression of it – *"You are our Father"* – we
insist upon that; You cannot disown us and, more than that,
we are the clay and You our Potter and we are all the work
of Your hand. O, what a word is this! It seems audacious
thus to throw the responsibility on God, and then with the

utmost intensity and vividness to say, *"Be not wroth very sore, O Lord, neither remember iniquity forever. Behold, see, we beseech You – **we are all Your people.**"*

Do you catch the spirit of this Scripture? Do you note its deep significance? To the writer it is an admission of the responsibility of the Creator, and that admission carries with it a promise of final good to every creature, so that I do not marvel at all, nor is there any tax made upon my faith, when I am told that *"the whole creation"* (Romans 8:22) shall ultimately be delivered, and *"every creature"* (Revelation 5:13) shall finally praise God.

He is *my* Redeemer; redemption is a part of creation; creation is still in progress; the Creator is the *sole* responsible party for the final outcome; and thus we may commit ourselves to God in all circumstances and with the utmost confidence, as to *"a faithful Creator."*

This *is* THE TRUE BASIS OF REDEMPTION – God our Creator, responsible for His Own creation, and every attribute of His Being pledged to its successful completion. God is able, and He will. The creature may rest secure on that basis, his *sole plea in every time of need*, and the all sufficient ground and full assurance of his deliverance and final triumph being – *"I AM YOURS."*

Your Part

Now that you have read this book, it's your turn.

If the truths presented here have helped you, don't let these truths die in your hands.

Please write to us and let us know your thoughts concerning its content.

Consider assisting us in getting this book into the hands of those who would be encouraged and strengthened by its message:

- Recommend it to your friends and loved ones.

- Order additional copies to give as gifts.

- Keep extra copies on hand to loan to others.

If you have not read the author's other works, order them today.

We would be honored to have your fellowship in getting this book freely to those who hunger spiritually. We have daily opportunities to send it to pastors, Sunday school teachers, Bible college professors and students, Bible class teachers, and prisoners.

Other Great Titles Available on the subject of THE SALVATION OF ALL and Related Themes:

All in All: The Goal of the Universe (#6269) by A.E. Knoch. (1874-1965). 222 pages, PB.

Ancient History of Universalism (#1926) by Hosea Ballou. 326 pages, PB.

At The End of the Ages: The Abolition of Hell (#3331) by Bob Evely. 171 pages, PB.

Bible Proofs of Universal Salvation (#2895) by J.W. Hanson. 107 pages, PB.

Bible Student's Notebook: Salvation OF All (SET) (#8302) by Clyde L. Pilkington, Jr. 52 pages, 8½" X 11", NB.

Bible Threatenings Explained: Or *Passages of Scripture Sometimes Quoted to Prove Endless Punishment Shown to Teach Consequences of Limited Duration* (#2965) by J.W. Hanson. 209 pages, PB.

Christ Triumphant, Or Universalism Asserted (#2264) by Thomas Allin. 327 pages, PB.

Death, Resurrection, Immortality (#2052) by Joseph E. Kirk. 111 pages, PB.

Destined for Salvation: God's Promise to Save Everyone (#3173) by Kalen Fristad. 157 pages, PB.

Endless Punishment: In the Very Words of Its Advocates (#7888) by Thomas J. Sawyer (1804-1899). 145 pages, NB.

Eonian: Everlasting or Age-Lasting? (#7673) complied by G.H. Todd. 47 pages, BK.

Eternal Torment, or Universal Reconciliation (#5601) by A.E. Knoch (1874- 1965). 51 pages, BK.

Every Knee Shall Bow: The Case for Christian Universalism (#4510) by Thomas Allin & Mark T. Chamberlain. 123 pages, PB.

God Does Not Foreclose: The Universal Promise of Salvation (#5202) by David L. Watson. 160 pages, PB.

God's Eonian Purpose (#3554) by Adlai Loudy. 383 pages, PB.

Greek Word AION - AIONIOS, Translated Everlasting - Eternal, The (#6562) by John Wesley Hanson. 79 pages, BK.

HELL, or "Pure from the blood of all men" (#6248) by Charles H. Welch. 57 pages, BK.

Hope Beyond Hell: The Righteous Purpose Of God's Judgment. (#4225) by Gerry Beauchemin. 247 pages, PB.

Humanity in the Arms of a Loving Savior (#4508) by James T. Burson. 68 pages, BK.

If God Could Save Everyone, WOULD HE?? (#4113) by Dr. Stephen E. Jones. 36 pages, BK.

Inescapable Love of God, The (#1814) by Thomas Talbott. 223 pages, PB.

Legend of Hell, The: An Examination of the Idea of Everlasting Punishment (#2235) by Percy Dearmer (1867-1936). 144 pages, 8½" X 11", NB.

Martin Zender Goes To Hell (#6494) by Martin Zender. 78 pages, PB.

Modern History of Universalism, The (#2079) by Thomas Whittemore (1800-1861). 458 pages, HB.

One Purpose of God, The: *An Answer to the Doctrine of Eternal Punishment* (#1816) by J. Bonda. 278 pages, PB.

Outcome of Infinite Grace (#6388) by Loyal F. Hurley. 62 pages, BK.

The Really Bad Thing About Free Will (#2250) by Martin Zender. 80 pages, PB.

Restitution of All Things (#3286) by Andrew Jukes. 194 pages, PB.

Restitution of All Things, The (#5175) by G.R. Hawtin. 47 pages, BK.

Restoration Of All Things, The: or Vindication of the Goodness and Grace of God. A (#2084) by Jeremiah White. 88 pages, 8½" x 11" PB.

Resurrection Of The Body, The (#1375) by E.W. Bullinger. 16 Pages, BK.

Rich Man and Lazarus, The (#7495) by Alan Burns. 30 pages, BK.

Rich Man and Lazarus, The (#6298) by Otis Q Sellers. 48 pages, BK.

Rich Man and Lazarus, The: *The Intermediate State* (#3127) by E.W. Bullinger. 64 pages, PB.

Salvation of the Unbeliever (#9125) by A.E. Knoch (1874-1965). 20 pages, BK.

Salvator Mundi: Is Christ the Saviour of All Men? (#6219) by Samuel Cox (1826-1893). 256 pages, PB.

Saviour of All Mankind (#3053) Compilation. 48 pages, BK.

Spirits In Prison, The (#1450) by E.W. Bullinger. A Study of (I Peter 3:17 – 4:6). 29 pages, BK.

Time and Eternity: A Biblical Study (#4209) by G.T. Stevenson. 76 pages, BK

Treatise on Atonement: The Final Reconciliation Of All Men (#1733) by Hosea Ballou. (8" x 11") PB.

Two Studies on Heaven and Hell (#7979) by A.E. Knoch (1874-1965). 27 pages, BK.

Union: or A Treatise of the Consanguinity and Affinity Between Christ and His Church (#2085) James Relly (1722-1778). 42 pages, 8½" x 11" PB.

Universal Restoration (#4134) by Elhanan Winchester (1751-1797). 72 pages, PB.

Universal Salvation? The Current Debate (#3591) by Thomas Talbott and others. 291 pages, PB.

Voice To Universalists (#2999) by Hosea Ballou. 8" x 11", PB.

What Does the Bible Say About Hell? *Wrestling with the Traditional View* (#1815) by Randy Klassen. 144 pages, PB.

www.URQA.com

Universal Reconciliation

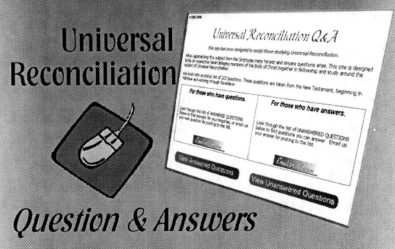

Question & Answers

A website designed to assist those studying Universal Reconciliation.

When approaching this subject from the Scriptures many honest and sincere questions arise. This site is designed to be an interactive forum bringing members of the Body of Christ together in fellowship and study around the subject of Universal Reconciliation.

We start with an initial list of 322 questions. These questions are taken from the New Testament, beginning in Matthew and working through Revelation.

For those who have questions:

Look through a list of ANSWERED QUESTIONS to find answers for your inquiries, or email us your own question for posting to the list.

For those who have answers:

Look through a list of UNANSWERED QUESTIONS to find questions you can answer. Email us your answers for posting to the list.

Stop by www.urqa.com
Today!

BOOKS BY:

CLYDE L. PILKINGTON, JR

Believer's Warfare, The: Wearing the Armor of Light in the Darkness of this World

(#7000) The believer is in the middle of an ancient spiritual warfare that is as old as mankind. The battle itself, although intense, is not complicated. It is not a process of spiritual hoop-jumping. Indeed it is simple. The Believer's Warfare surveys a few key passages of Scripture to reveal God's sure plan of victory in the life of His saints. 48 pages, BK.

Bible Student's Notebook, The (VOLUMES)

The Bible Student's Notebook is a periodical dedicated to the: - Promotion of Bible study - Encouragement of the believer's growth in grace - Support of the role of family patriarch - Recovery of truth that has too long been hidden under the veils of traditionalism, prejudice, misunderstanding and fear. The Bible Student's Notebook is not connected with any "Church," "Movement," "Organization," "Society," "Mission," or separate body of believers, but is sent forth to and for all of God's saints. Available in Paperback Volumes.

Church in Ruins, The: Brief Thoughts on II Timothy

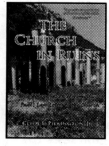

(#3325) This brief survey of Paul's last epistle will reveal that while almost 2000 years have transpired, the condition of the church has remained the same, and indeed has worsened in accordance with Paul's warning to Timothy. This book is not a call for a re-awakening of "the church," because it is apparent that this is not Father's plan. Rather, it is a call to individual men – men whose place in the Christian religious system has left them empty, stagnant, and restless – to awaken to Father's call to be His faithful servant and stand outside of that system to look for other faithful men as well. 128 pages, PB.

Due Benevolence: A Study of Biblical Sexuality

(#3775) Think you have read all that there is on the subject of sexuality from the Bible? Think again! Religious moralists have taken the wonderful gift of human beauty and sexuality and made them something dirty and sinful. Much is at stake regarding truth, as well as the nature and character of God Himself. A groundbreaking work providing…

• A refreshingly honest and uninhibited look at sexuality.
• A breath of fresh air from the religious and Victorian mentality.
• A daring and valuable glimpse at the wonderful light just outside sexuality's prison-cell door. 220 pages, PB.

Heaven's Embassy: The Divine Plan & Purpose of the Home

(#5675) The home is central to all of God's dealings with man throughout the course of time. It is His Divine "institution" and "organization" upon the earth; and for the believer, it is the Embassy of Heaven. An embassy is "the residence or office of an ambassador." Since the believer is an ambassador of the Lord Jesus Christ (II Corinthians 5:14-21), his home is thus the Divine Embassy of heavenly ministry. Pauline ministry is centered in the homes of believers. This is even the true sphere  of the Body of Christ; for this reason our apostle speaks of "church in thy house." This book doesn't focus upon the external specifics of the ministry of Heaven's Embassy (such as hospitality); that will be saved for another volume. Instead, it looks at the inner-workings of the Embassy itself; focusing upon its very nature and internal purpose and function. 250 pages, PB.

I Choose! Living Life to Its Fullest

(#4120) Forty-Eight Daily Thoughts on Divine Life. You are alive! Yet not just alive, but alive with the very life of God! Don't allow your "What if…" imaginations of the past or the future to lay claim to the present that God has given you. Allow the objective, unchanging truth of who God has made you in the Lord Jesus Christ to transform your mind and life as you take this spiritual journey of "I Choose." 192 pages, PB.

Nothing Will Be Lost! The Truth About God's Good News

(#3750) This is an abridgement of the larger work The Salvation of All. It is designed as a give-away edition, with quantity pricing available. 88 pages, PB.

The Outsiders: God's Called-Out Ones – A Biblical Look at the Church – God's Ecclesia

(#4125) In 1995, after sixteen years of being in the "pastorate" the author walked away. He left the "religious system" by resigning from the very "church" and "ministry" he had formed. In many ways this work is a testament to these actions. This testimony was thirty years in the making -- the results of a spiritual journey that the author found to be common to other saints scattered throughout the world and across history. This is an opportunity to explain why some who love the Lord no longer "go to church." It does not seek to persuade others to do something different; but rather to simply be who and what they already are "in Him." This is an uncovering of the truth of the church, and an encouragement for the members of His Body to enjoy the position and standing "in Christ" that they already possess, realizing that they are truly "complete in Him" (Colossians 2:10), that He alone is their Life (Colossians 3:4), and that His Life is full of freedom (Galatians 5:1). 128 pages, PB.

Plowboy's Bible, The : God's Word for Common Man

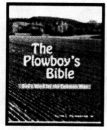

(#4425) Shocking conclusions from the man that brought you The King James Bible Song. This book represents years of study and a significant change in understanding. Raised on and trained in a "King James Only" position, most of the author's teaching ministry was centered on the defense of the KJV. He had early associations with major proponents of this position and their followers. He actively taught classes and seminars on the subject of Bible versions. For many years he distributed thousands of books from a collection of over 100 different titles in support of the KJV position. Here he shares what he has come to see that has caused him to completely abandon his former position. 254 pages, PB.

Salvation Of ALL, The: Creation's Final Destination (A Biblical Look at Universal Reconciliation)

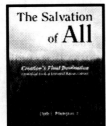

(#7001) The Gospel of our Lord and Savior, Jesus Christ is truly better "Good News" than we could ever have imagined. It is far more glorious than religion would ever have us believe. The Salvation of All is a book about a "Good News" that will reach its final goal in the salvation of all mankind. 262 pages, PB.

Suffering: God's Forgotten Gift

Two gifts given to the believer are mentioned by Paul in Philippians 1:29. The first is "to believe on Him." This is a glorious gift. Every believer has been given this gift from God. Those who possess it may not even fully recognize it as a gift from Him, but indeed faith is God's wonderful gift to us. Faith is a rich gift from God, but there is also another gift from God to the believer, mentioned by Paul in Philippians 1:29, that is equally as glorious. The second gift is "also to suffer for His sake."

This, too, is a glorious gift. Every believer has been given this gift from God as well, but those who possess it often do not fully recognize it for what it is. Indeed, suffering for His sake similarly is God's wonderful gift to us. Paul teaches us to embrace this second gift as well as we do the first! 100 pages, PB.

Daily Goodies: 365 Thoughts on Scriptural Truths

(#1747) This is a great resource for personal and family study, as well as a valuable reference volume covering many varied biblical themes. This is a collection of choice selections from the author's Daily E-mail Goodies. These free daily e-mails began being issued in 2003 and contain studies on scriptural themes. 490 pages, PB.

I Am! Who and What God Says I Am!
The Divine Reckoning of the Renewed Mind; Daily Thoughts on Divine Life

(#1737) People are always talking about their attempts to discover their true selves – of trying to "find themselves." The believer in the Lord Jesus Christ needs to find out who they *really* are. This doesn't need to be such a difficult search. All that is really needed is a careful look at the Scriptures, and a simple faith in the words of who and what God says we are. God knows who we are; all we need to do is to *believe Him*. This book catalogs the Divine Record of who and what God says that you are. It is a short encyclopedia of faith – the truth about you. It is the truth about you, simply because it is *God* Who has said it. God has spoken these truths concerning you – the *real* you. Believe His record! Refuse to be the shell of a person, pushed into a mold of Adamic conformity. Be the real you that God has uniquely designed you to be. Refuse to be bullied out of your divinely designed identity that our Father has given you. 107 pages, PB.

The King James Version – 400 Years of Bondage
1611-2011

(#4682) 1611 was not a high spiritual mark in the history of the church, the Body of Christ. Instead of being a grand year of the pinnacle of preservation or perfection of God's Word, it was rather the sad depths of the subtle corrupting of God's Word by the historic union of governmental and ecclesiastical politics. -- 72 pages, PB.

DAILY EMAIL GOODIES™

Do you receive our
Daily Email Goodies™?

These are free daily emails that contain short quotes, articles, and studies on Biblical themes.

These are the original writings of Clyde L. Pilkington, Jr, as well as gleanings from other authors.

Request to be added to our free
Daily Email Goodies™

If you would like to be added to the mailing list, email us at:

Goodies@StudyShelf.com

ENJOY BOOKS?

Visit us at:

www.StudyShelf.com

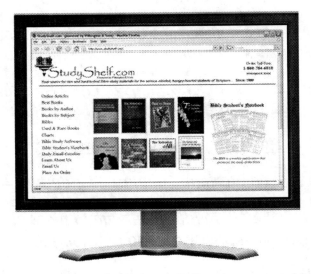

Over the years we have often been asked to recommend books. The requests come from believers who longed for material with substance. Study Shelf™ is a collection of books which are, in our opinion, the very best in print. Many of these books are "unknown" to the members of the Body of Christ at large, and most are not available at your local "Christian" bookstore.

YOU CAN:

Read:

A wealth of articles from past issues of the *Bible Student's Notebook*

Purchase:

Rare and hard to find books, booklets, leaflets, Bibles, etc. in our 24/7 online store.